PRAISE FOR ALLISON

This book dares the reader to examine their perception on issues that are very relevant to the times and culture we live in. It is written by an author who has earned the right to speak out of the painful and powerful journey she and her husband have walked with the Lord, learning how to effectively love beyond their ability to understand at times, yet not being willing to separate themselves from the struggles their son faced.

We salute your willingness to love the lonely and confused in the "liminal spaces," and we thank you for sharing the challenge this presents to the millennial church.

May God guide us all.

LINDA ROWETT
Director of Hope Trust Ireland

PARENTING THE RAINBOW

A CHRISTIAN PARENT'S GUIDE TO LOVING THEIR GAY CHILD WELL

ALLISON ZIMMERMAN

Copyright © 2022 by Allison Zimmerman

All rights reserved.

No part of this book may be reproduced in any form or by any electronic or mechanical means, including information storage and retrieval systems, without written permission from the author, except for the use of brief quotations in a book review.

Unless otherwise marked, Scripture quotations are taken from the New King James Version®. Copyright © 1982 by Thomas Nelson. Used by permission. All rights reserved.

Scripture quotations marked TPT are from The Passion Translation®. Copyright © 2017, 2018, 2020 by Passion & Fire Ministries, Inc. Used by permission. All rights reserved. ThePassionTranslation.com.

Scripture quotations marked AMP are from the Amplified Bible. Copyright © 2015 by The Lockman Foundation, La Habra, CA 90631. All rights reserved.

Scripture quotations marked MSG are taken from *THE MESSAGE*, copyright © 1993, 2002, 2018 by Eugene H. Peterson. Used by permission of NavPress. All rights reserved. Represented by Tyndale House Publishers, Inc.

Scripture quotations marked NIV are from THE HOLY BIBLE, NEW INTERNATIONAL VERSION®, NIV® Copyright © 1973, 1978, 1984, 2011 by Biblica, Inc.® Used by permission. All rights reserved worldwide.

Cover art and design: Rob Zimmerman

Cover photo credit: Mike Cruz

Interior design: Rich Bullock – www.perilousfiction.com

V - 9/17/22 - 1

*To my patient husband Rob, who made space
and silence for me to create in,
and for Rainbow Parents everywhere.
You are seen, the struggle is real.
I bless you to find the path of love for your situation.*

CONTENTS

Foreword	xi
Introduction	xiii
1. Coming Out	1
2. My Kid?	9
3. Love Covers	19
4. Help!	25
5. When…	29
6. Same Sex Attraction	37
7. Our dilemma	41
8. What Is Love?	49
9. Real vs. Fake	55
10. Mine vs. Yours	61
11. The Church	67
12. Life Goes On	77
13. What About The Wedding?	83
14. Further Thoughts	89
15. Conclusions	97
Afterword	105
Author Note	109
Discussion Questions	111
Recommendations for Further Reading	117
Acknowledgments	119
About the Author	121
Also by Allison Zimmerman	123

*A physician once said,
"The best medicine
for humans is love."
Someone asked,
"What if it doesn't work?"
He smiled and said,
"Increase the dose."*

— UNKNOWN

FOREWORD

LYLE WELLS

I had the pleasure of meeting Allison at a pastor's conference—she approached me after one of my teaching sessions, and I was immediately struck by her sincere heart, the depth of her love and faith in Jesus, and her transparency as she opened up her life to me. During my keynote, I had referenced the fact that my wife and I have been in a unique relationship: a ministry family walking with our son, a gay man.

What I encountered that day is what you will encounter as you read through the pages of this book. You will hear her story in a very personal way, and she will share many practical lessons that she has learned throughout this journey.

You will see a woman, a wife, a mother who is both refreshingly candid and incredibly courageous.

When this journey began for my wife and I, we found very few relevant resources. Few of my peers in ministry were comfortable or capable of having a deep conversation around this topic. Many of the ministry resources available at the time focused on how to confront and convict our son, or they offered up unrealistic scenarios, typically involving the prodigal son story. As we were preparing for one particularly critical conversation with our son, I told my wife, "I feel like we are going to battle armed with a butter knife."

In my conversations with Allison, I know she felt much the same way, and that is why you are holding this book. She has brilliantly written it in a way that feels like a conversation with a trusted friend. A friend who brings hope, guidance, wisdom, community, and clarity.

One of the truths we all experience is that when we become anxious, we seek safety. Our desire is to find a safe place and a safe person. I believe that in these pages many of you will find this book to be a safe place and Allison Zimmerman to be one of your safe people. I certainly did.

My prayers are with you and all others who are reading this book and walking this path.

On Purpose,
Lyle Wells
President, Integrus Leadership

INTRODUCTION
NATHAN EDWARDSON

I write these thoughts from a coffee shop in Norway.

It's Pride Week. Summer break has just begun, and it happens to be the hottest day of the year. Thousands of youth flood the city streets. I'm drinking a cappuccino and scrolling through Instagram, taking advantage of the coffeehouse Wi-Fi. Across the street I see a Pride flag hung boldly in a business window—the largest Pride flag I've seen in my life. I've seen these flags all day, draped and displayed throughout the city. Rainbows everywhere.

We've just learned about a mass shooting in Oslo city center. Two shot dead and twenty-one injured. The deadliest shooting in Norway since 2011. I'm shocked. My daughter Adiah and I rode scooters through that very city center earlier that day. The news tells us this was a targeted attack against the gay community. My wife, who hears about the shooting back home, sends me a text to see if we're OK.

INTRODUCTION

Our hearts break. It feels so close, so personal. We feel angry and helpless.

Later that night, the Norwegian Prime Minister makes a statement, "The shooting in the night put an end to the Pride Parade, but it will not stop our fight and efforts to fight discrimination, prejudice, and hatred."

I struggle to fall asleep.

How we respond to the LGBTQ community is potentially one of the most divisive issues in today's society, let alone in the church. Yet in this tension, God is raising up healthy Spirit-filled voices. We live in a day like no other, and we, as followers of Jesus, must lead the way.

Parenting the Rainbow brings us into the heart cry and love of a mom for her gay son.

Through her own voyage into the fearless and shame-free space of love, presence, and embrace, Allison Zimmerman takes us on a joy-drenched, pain-filled journey of parenting in the twenty-first century.

Parenting the Rainbow offers stunning wisdom for parents, or anyone navigating the nuance of today's culture, family, and sexuality. One of the most honest, authentic souls I've ever met, Allison shows us how to walk deeply not only with God but with our gay sons and daughters. This non-religious memoir is honest, refreshing, and challenging to the core for those brave enough to ask hard questions, listen to God, and learn anew how to love like Jesus. A must-read for anyone wanting to cultivate deep and lasting relationships with sons and daughters.

While many in the church are passive or distant at best,

INTRODUCTION

especially when it comes to sexuality, this book is an invitation into extravagant love.

I've asked this question for years: "How come we are silent about sexuality in the two places we need it the most—in the church and in the home?" Yet God is cultivating fathers and mothers after His own heart. Parents so deeply secure in who they are, they can help others discover who they are. Fearless, present, honest, and authentic. Never has our generation needed these mothers and fathers more.

As someone who longs for God's heart for the LGBTQ community, I too need this book.

Finally, honest conversations matter now more than ever. May we have the courage needed to engage the talks, the tension, and the treasure of the LGBTQ community, that we might somehow grasp deeply the very heart of God.

Let's follow Jesus wholeheartedly, the One who loves far deeper and greater than we could ever imagine.

Nathan Edwardson
The Stirring Church
Redding, California

PARENTING THE RAINBOW

1

COMING OUT

It was a balmy day in the tropics. The trade winds were blowing. Maybe a storm was even on the horizon, judging by the way the wind drove the waves. Little did we know that our comfortable, safe world was about to be invaded by the winds of change with one communication.

A simple (or not so simple) message from our precious son.

We were driving home from a Christmas bazaar. Local vendors selling their wares—Christmas ornaments, earrings, a book on the history of our beloved island. A lovely day. We were thankful and excited about the upcoming season, the things God had for us, and what He might allow us to partner with Him in.

On the way home, my inbox pinged. I was excited to hear from my boy, who was in college in the US. A simple and said I did not want to talk about it but that when the news became public, I wanted them to have heard it from me. One of those that I told was able to park their curiosity and let me find my own slow way forward. I appreciate their willingness to hold what questions they might have, giving me space to answer some of my own without having to take care of what was theirs in the process of learning what was mine.

Our son following a gay lifestyle would probably mean no little nerdy kids would carry his DNA in the future. I had to die to the idea of traditional grandchildren from this dear one. This was a point of grief. Some may call it selfish, but it is part of the price of the package. I was also afraid for his health. Again, some may believe this was unfounded, but it was my reality.

Maybe you are grappling with your kids' choices. Aching over their wishes and the fact that you see things so differently. Our perspectives differ so vastly! We may be shocked, angry, in denial, or just unable to conceive of what we have been told. Maybe we feel our child is "exploring," that he will figure things out. However, by the time we are aware and in the loop, we needs must remember that "this ship has already left the harbor." After taking a breath, the big thing we need to do is choose love. Love is the only sane choice, the only reasonable alternative to a whole world of hate that we have often thrown at people who choose other than our biblical worldview.

There are a few things to keep in mind as you read this book. You may be reading it looking for answers, or you might be looking to criticize the way we handled things.

Either way, I am sure you will find areas where we could have done better. Perhaps you're here because you are in the same boat as we were and know the angst that I describe. May we know the Lord's peace as we process and walk this part of our journey. Wherever we are at, for whatever reason you have picked up this book, all I can say is that rightly or wrongly, this is our story, our account. We have probably done some things wrong in other people's estimation, and we may have done some things right. In fact, what you will read is just a few chapters of our story, as it is still being written. We continue to learn and we continue to love.

My son first came out to one of his sisters. At that time, they shared an Apple ID, and some questionable material was showing up on her device. She figured this was a mistake and spoke with her brother. When my daughter found out, it was largely information that she held with her husband and one other. She was advised to "keep the secret," that it was my son's news to tell...so she kept the secret, but not without personal cost. She needed her community too. To be isolated by that level of knowledge within the context of a very close family...that took its toll. She bore the burden of silence in her role as sister. Meanwhile, I lived in my world "as usual," with no idea that everything had changed or was about to change with one announcement. Oblivion in action!

In family we come together, whatever needs to be said and known. Our truth can bring us closer even if we are divided in the details.

Maybe you find yourself in the role of secret keeper.

Possibly, like others who have been there, you are terrified at what might be ahead. Afraid of what the future might be like as you hold new knowledge concerning your beloved son or daughter.

How can we support someone to come out to their significant others?

Are we able to take a step back and ask ourselves, "What is mine versus what is theirs?" Can we care for our dear ones with compassion as they share what has been a closely held secret for many years? Maybe we have been hurt by the way others have handled our own situations. There may be conflicting codes of ethics involved as you listen to a worldview that is different than yours but try to hold true to what your values are.

I love what one friend did. When she saw a family member in a compromising situation, she had a "heart to heart" with her and said, "Either you tell, or I do. You have until such-and-such a time to do so." This kind of loving reaction gives the individual with the secret a nudge toward the opportunity to speak up and out for themselves. If kids we know are getting "found out," it is time for us to help them voice where they are at and come out to the people that are important to them.

Offering to go with someone as they take the brave leap to speak out to their families is powerful. Remember, this is not easy for our offspring or for us. Our kids are taking a huge risk! We as Christians are not always well known for having a loving reaction when faced with something we have labeled as sin. Back in the day, teen pregnancy was the hot button topic we were wrestling with. I have seen families turned upside down because of such: Girl gets pregnant, guy gets to go on and live his life, girl's family is shattered. If dad works for the church, he might lose his job because he is deemed incapable of controlling his own house...we have come a long way, but we are not there yet!

If our child comes out to us, he/she is exhibiting great trust. If they are Christian, they have prayed about this, labored over it, wrestled with it, struggled, sought outside counsel about it. They have tried every available thing they know: Asking God to take away the gay, hiding in plain sight because they are painfully aware that our understanding of the Scriptures condemns them. Brave is the one who comes forward—he/she has to exercise a whole lot of trust in those they come out to.

At this stage in our experience, it might be a good time to ask our loving heavenly Father for a word from His heart to our situation, perhaps a Scripture, a verse, or a song. What is Father saying to us right now when our world is wobbling? An anchor for our soul to stabilize us in spirit so that we can hang on to the heart of our child as we hang on to Father's love toward us while we navigate the waters ahead.

~

PLEASE NOTE that there are discussion questions at the end of the book for deeper engagement with the material in each chapter.

2

MY KID?

Many years ago, fortuitously, someone asked me, "What would you do if one of your kids was gay?" In an off-the-cuff way I quipped back, "I'd love them. Your kid is your kid, nothing changes that."

I am grateful for this interaction that God used to prepare my heart. Thankful that our instinct can be to love, not judge, to care for and to come alongside. The choices of one child will force other children to make decisions for their families. We must beware, if there are other kids in the house, that their lives and stories matter too. It would be so easy to hyper-focus on one child while others are being overlooked. How many special occasions have been hijacked because we didn't have the bandwidth to support all of our children exactly where they were at? Parent, let's not neglect one child as we try to support another!

Siblings with kids may be asking when and how to

them in the loving hands of our Lord, let them go in His love, trusting that He will in His time and space meet with them in powerful ways, leading them closer to His heart and plans for their lives? Should this not be our stance with all of our children?

As Christians we tend to grade sin. We know this. We even talk about the fact that we do this as if we are those who are above it. Yet we still fall prey to the practice of selective sin structures. What are your big three? We all have them. When we were missionaries on the island of Kiribati, the big three prohibitions were "no smoking, no drinking, no dancing." It may seem ludicrous to us that the last of these was what made the cut, but it was what it was. Jesus operated so differently than us. He Who was friend of sinners, companion of the lost.

From this base, we may find ourselves facing a dichotomy because our gay children often no longer see their lifestyle choices as sin. Our kids may have been raised in an ultra-orthodox or conservative home, and yet their desires are taking them far from the narrow confines in which we reared them.

This is an electronic information age. Where in the past the family investment in an encyclopedia was a ready source of knowledge, nowadays one's peers or a podcast provide the answers being sought, and God knows how misleading simple searches on the internet can be at times! Just try a simple search on weight loss and see what wild and wacky suggestions come forth! Without a doubt there is a generation gap as we grapple with what might be hard things in our family. Parents, we may not know where to turn, while our kids have a whole wealth of information at the tips of their fingers.

My prayer is that our kids will find His wisdom. Parent, child, may neither of us prove to be locked into being those who value our ego or sense of being right at the expense of the heart of the relationship we share. Let us pray for our children to encounter God and His Wisdom and let Father sort out the details.

As parents, we may not have done that well in loving our kids. We grew up with the concept of tough love, which can have such harsh consequences. Let us not get stuck on either end of the spectrum, for there can be error in the edges. May we walk with Christ as we come to the conclusion of love and learn how to love well for our family. If we have this chance to remain in our kid's life, let's not be those who waste our miracle. Let us not squander the good of our relationship.

Often dads want to come up with a plan and moms want to protect their kids. Grandparents may want to quote the Bible. We wonder "what we did wrong." Parents, we are not to blame for this. We hope and pray our kids don't leave the community of faith, but often the church does not know what to do with our gay children. So much swirls around in our brain when we are trying to make sense of where we are at in our experience as we ponder this complex knot and the clash of desire.

Jesus was all about unity. He was not afraid of hard conversations that needed to be had. He engaged those who had legitimate questions. It was the religious that did not fare so well in the courts He held. Where do we fall?

Are we stuck in excessive grace or ultra-legalism? Do we stand in judgment, or can we show mercy? Because the last time I looked, "mercy triumphs over judgment" (James 2:13). May we land with Jesus as we tenderly care for the hearts of our kids. May He use our story for His glory!

It seems we are in a world of post-Christian thinking. God have mercy if we and the nations we come from feel we have outgrown the need for His hand of love on our lives. Everything is up for discussion...we need to be solid on which side of the Word of God we land on, and like Paul said, "may the Lord make these things clear to you" (Philippians 3:15, loosely translated Allison version). Cancel culture is a buzzword, and we the church led the way into this dark vein. Are we guilty of being a society who throws away anything that messes with our metric, all the while click-clacking our heels down the cloistered hallways of our familiar institutions?

Nevertheless, here we find ourselves. You may say, "How can two walk together unless they be agreed?" (Amos 3:3). Such a good question! Find what you can agree on, walk there, while hopefully both parties remain soft-hearted enough to let Jesus into the areas where there is difference and confusion.

I realize there is potential kickback from protagonist and antagonist alike. This might not be a message people want to hear on either side of the discussion. Our call is to "...love one another, for love is of God and everyone who loves is born of God" (1 John 4:7, NKJV). What will your love look like? Hopefully, we will love like Him, above and beyond the call of duty. Oh, the love of God that finds us when we are lost and never quits on us! We have been recipients of such kindness, yet are so stingy in returning the favor to those around us. May we be those who leave no vacuum of love that might send our child wandering and wondering what might fill the holes we have left vacant.

Your kid is your kid. This one who concerns you, the child you have nurtured and raised, who has changed your world by a courageous announcement. Do you know how hard it is for gay kids to trust their Christian parents? To come out to the ones who raised them? Our kids know the traditional Judeo-Christian thinking on homosexuality. They were spoon-fed our theology, they learned what we believe around the dinner table and in casual conversation. Some of us need to go back with a humble heart and repent (finger pointing back at self) for the way we have spoken, joked, or reacted to people in the gay community.

When our kids are attempting to come out to us, they are faced with telling us news that they feel could shatter our world. With speaking words that most likely will rock our realities. How they have labored over telling us something we might not want to hear! This wasn't a simple process. Your child had to think and plan with much deliberation in advance, knowing what is about to transpire within the family is not easy on either party.

From the child's perspective, the parents "won't be into" what they are about to hear. Our son told us when he was older and out of the house. He didn't want to be sent to "conversion camp," a place where he felt he would be "reprogrammed" to think differently or have an exorcism from the demon spirits he might have picked up along the way. He wanted to be gay. He had felt this way for many years, and he had seen us love, embrace, honor and work with people in all phases of their journey. He didn't want to change, neither did he want to be kicked out of our family.

Our kids know how we perceive the world and the question of homosexuality. Coming forward with their truth, which in the eyes of parents, siblings, grandparents, family members may be considered a lie, they are sharing something that could be divisive. Our child runs the risk of being condemned for their choices, yet can we accept them with the same love we have held in our hearts for these many years? As we pray, we remember that we all make choices, every one of them carrying a consequence. May God guard and guide us all in every scenario we find ourselves so that we—parents and children—choose well.

We as parents need to realize that what's ours to deal with is ours, and what's theirs is theirs. We must deal with and clean up our side of the street while we pray for our child in his/her place of walking through this season of their lives. We must do our own individual work. The only person we can change is ourselves, the only mind we can change is our own. When love wins, some of the details just don't seem as important as they once used to, when we let go of our selfish desire for the child in our image and receive the good of the child we have. This is not a problem for us to fix, it is the life we are living.

Parent, you are not alone! This is not the end of your world. There are worse things than this. You will survive!

You can love through this and come out closer to Jesus and the depths of His love, knowing Him more as a result of this journey being entrusted to you.

Let us remember that we might not want to land permanently where we are at when we first hear "the news." Maybe we need space to process, to love, care, and pray. Our issues are ours, those of our child belong to them. We cannot change them by bashing them over the head with doctrine, nor will they change us with a gospel of license and liberation. Where we start, we may not want to finish. We need to seek the Lord as we bring our family to His attention, asking Him how we navigate the road ahead. Where can we agree? Are there areas we cannot come together? How can we move forward in love?

When a child comes out as gay in today's society, there is much acceptance from the world or their peers, but what about the people they grew up with? Their choices challenge the ideals we have instilled in them of manhood, womanhood, traditional nuclear families. Salvation is contested. Cultural Christian norms are called into question...can our present-day understanding handle the incongruence of how we wish things were versus how they seem to be? We have to figure out how to move forward into the new realities thrust upon our family unit.

Information that has blindsided us is news our child has grappled with and had much longer to process. They are coming to us with part of their truth, a part we may not like or appreciate. How deep is our love, dear parent? What will we allow to divide us from our child? Will we love them more than those to whom he/she will run? Will we drive them deeper into where they are heading by our lack of compassion and hardness of heart, by our need to control every outcome? When something of this nature rocks our reality, it is time to lean on the Rock of Ages, to hide out in Him until He gives us the plan forward. How will He lead and guide? He seeks and saves, what do we want to do? Where do we want to land with our kids? To drive them away or draw them near?

The parent of a trans child once told me, "The more I prayed, the more I was the one who was changed." In the discussion among the church family, I realize this is such a nuanced issue. Son/daughter, remember you have changed the family conversation, now may space be given as we wrestle through the hard questions with God and one another. Peace for the process! Peace as we all process.

3

LOVE COVERS

Love covers. Parents, love your children! Love your kids more than their peers, more than any other influencer in their life. Let your love for them be tangible. Don't throw the Bible at them—they probably know the six or seven passages that pertain to homosexuality better than you do.

The gap we face is not about knowledge, it's about understanding. We don't understand how our child has landed where they have, and our offspring has trouble understanding how we have ever believed the things we do. Let us learn to love in the tension of unfinished answers. In the liminal place, the place where the rub is.

We need to keep loving through the angst to reach a place where we can both be seen and heard, not condemned or standing in judgment. May we both have the grace to "really listen" when the other speaks, not listening to confirm bias but listening to hear one another's hearts. We might learn something!

When we received the Facebook message of my son's coming out, we knew we loved him and we expressed our love. We also knew we didn't understand where he was coming from and that we had to take a breath...my son says, "It was a very long breath." It took me about a week to find my feet and re-engage in conversation. Take the time you need, time that heals, not divides. Time to bring you back together.

What was a long week for my son was a week of me sitting with Jesus. As I sat, he waited alone in his college dorm in a different country. How would we love him? Would we love him going forward with the information we now had? It is OK for us to tell our kids we need space to digest what is ahead. They have known about this a long time—catching up can be a beastly job! It's alright for us to need space to sort our brains out, to think clearly as we process the news that has been shared with us.

My son said to me that he advises kids coming out to build strong community as it will make it easier for them if their parents don't take it too well...folks, let us love more. Doesn't this just grieve our heart? Our kids are expecting a bad reaction from us. They realize that we talk a good game about loving unconditionally...until they come out as gay. My prayer and challenge is that I will love all of my children well enough that I don't drive them away for any reason. May we look for answers as we grapple with this together.

Churches typically have been clumsy in loving the "gay

among them." We have navigated around homosexuality, treating it as a topic and not a real and relevant part of people's lives, often steering clear of contact because where gay people are at messes with our religion. Do we think it will "rub off" on us? We are often afraid of what we don't understand.

Parents, pastors, is it possible that our gay kids' choices are kicking stuff up in us? If we have come from a traditional background, we have certain expectations. We want to believe everyone will grow up to be and do certain things and, of course, love the Lord with all their hearts, yet sometimes our "what is" differs from the way we wish things were. We have to do our own work. Does this kick up things from our past, even our religious past? Is there unfinished business we need to take care of? Does this question who we are as a family? Does this challenge your manhood, Dad? Mom, do you wonder if there was something wrong with the way you cuddled your kid? This is unnerving to us. What is being hit on in you? Do we blame the other parent? The family ancestry? The youth pastor? Do we blame what could be generational sin? We ask, "Where did we go wrong?"

Pastor, do you want to preach away the gay, pretend it doesn't exist, reduce the homosexual's ability to be in community? Oh, we are so complex! We want someone to pay for what we are going through, and it would be easier if there was someone or something to blame that wasn't us…parent, we must take care of what is ours and not put that on the shoulders of our child. Preacher, how will you lead your people in love? We have to work through our own stuff, bearing in mind that where we are right now might not be where we eventually land.

We had to work through knowing our child waited till he was out of the house to come out because he was unsure of the outcome, yet he still wanted to honor us by not dating until he had told us the news. That he'd wanted to be out of the house so that if it didn't go well, he would have options, a Plan B. That he was afraid we'd send him to conversion camp. What we need in this day and age is conversation camp! We need to come together with our stories, to learn from one another.

Early on, a wise woman suggested I asked my son if, when I came to passages in the Word that I saw differently than him, he would be willing to discuss them with me. Could there be room for discourse? (My son agreed to this possibility—he wanted to talk about it with us.) Can we engage with our kids in the difference? Engage them, not just throw Bible verses at them?

Authoritarianism in the home, thankfully, seems to be dying, and if it isn't, it will kill us all! The way we might have been raised is not the mode of the day. What is more important? For us to cast judgment, or to come together with a willingness to hear, learn, and love? We want to foster understanding one with another, not an adversarial stance. Affirming that "you will always be my son/daughter," assuring them that will never change. Moving forward in ways that promote relationship, not rejection from either parent or child.

This topic, for some, questions the family ideals of masculinity and femininity, manhood and womanhood (for goodness' sake, much needs to be questioned concerning the latter!) We have come a long way as a society, but there is yet a ways to go! Within the parameters of this conversation, cultural norms are called into question. We have our new normal to figure out. We don't like change. Sometimes we run from the challenge of growth. What needs to happen in us, in our family, to get us where God wants us? How do we all as individuals need to respond at the foot of the cross as we find our center in the new norm? There is room for all of us to grow as we come closer to God and hopefully one another. Wouldn't it be wonderful if our contending with what we now face makes us purer expressions of the love of Christ for a lost and dying world?

One thing I would really say is: Let us encourage our child to stay in the Word. We need to do likewise! Not building a doctrine for or against an issue based on six or seven passages. Let us all stay open to Him in this new season. Not going to the Word for ammunition for or against the subject of homosexuality, but going to the Word as a gateway to God and His love for us.

When my boy agreed that he would be willing to discuss our differences, one might think I had an opening to go right to business in moral debate. It is so interesting to me that "those Scriptures" have never come up since his big reveal...God knows the time and place for us to engage all of our questions in safety and love. Friends said a Scripture they held onto throughout their journey was "We do not know what to do, but our eyes are on You" (2 Chronicles 20:12 NIV). What a gift, that we don't have to have everything figured out, just keep our eyes on the One Who knows the end from the beginning!

There are few resources out there, however we need to be careful what we read, what we fill our minds with. If we gorge ourselves with material that reeks of judgment or condemnation, we will be more likely to fall on that end of the spectrum. Beware of who or what informs your minds within this critical time in the life of your family as you find your identity, albeit as a household in flux.

We as parents might feel blindsided by this news, and we have to learn to live with the tensions that may be oozing out of this new reality. We may feel we are groping in the dark, all the while wanting to land on the side of love. Can we love enough to recognize we can disagree without rejection? There are many other things we might not agree with our kids on—hairstyles, hem length, body art. We have all lived through acrimonious elections that divided friends and families. There are many things we choose to see differently, but can we still choose to love? Can we put aside the debate about where we went wrong and listen to the still small voice what whispers truth to our heart?

My prayer is that we will always land on the side of love, but in so doing, not exclude the discussion of truth, remembering that a discussion is not a monologue, not a one-sided loop from parent or child. May our ears and hearts be open to where God wants us to land in this adventure into which we have been birthed.

4

HELP!

When this hits your family, it hits hard. It isn't going away, and we as parents are not quite sure where we will land. The kid we raised is not the person we thought we had raised. What exactly do we believe anyway? My aim here is not to tell you how to think but to let you in on our current family portrait. Again, we have not done all things well, but we did our best with the facts we had, which I am sure is your hope as you read this book.

What should we even believe? It seems that the church at large is lost in this area. On the staff of any given place of worship, there might be varying opinions concerning homosexuality. It may be hard, in your time of searching and discovery, to get helpful answers. Ours is a unique call. Will we change our theology to match our reality? The struggle is with what we have believed versus the life we lead. Where will we land in this? When the church doesn't appear to have the answers we so desperately seek, we can be in danger of going to the world for their solutions. This is all at a time when we so deeply need community and connection but feel cut off from such because the reality of homosexuality and the church is such a loaded-gun issue. We find ourselves in a state of confusion.

Our circumstances have exiled and isolated us. We want to press stop, to change the channel, but like it or lump it, here we are. Our prayer becomes "Your will be done—not mine or theirs, but Yours, Lord!"

Our thinking has been challenged, and we are questioning things. Is it possible that some of our thinking needs to be put under the microscope of His love for fresh inspection? Perhaps it's a time to submit our notions and beliefs to Him once again, ask Him for more, for what He might have us learn in this new world we are facing. Have we ever looked into the Word for ourselves, or have we blindly accepted the word of another on the subject of homosexuality? May we not just settle for the words of those who are disconnected from the trails we tread. Pharisaical thinking, be silenced! May we have space and grace to walk the path ahead of us in the beauty and intimacy of our Lord.

Who is our God, and can He handle this? What will we do with what we don't agree with? Where will we land with what we don't understand? How will we live in the land of in-between, that liminal space, the margins, where questions loom larger than the answers that seem available. Our God is able, our God is enough. His love is bigger, broader, greater, and deeper. We can trust Him for our children. May we know His beauty from our ashes (Isaiah 61:3).

We need a hook for our faith. What can we believe for? Not what do we doubt, not the problem, our proposed solutions or anything else, but a safe landing place for our faith through trusting Him in the places we find ourselves. I like to immerse myself in the Word. Imperfect as I am, I get to deep dive with Jesus. He speaks, and I hang on for dear life through the things that might hit me on any given day. God shows up where the rubber hits the road, in our pain and our confusion. What we are currently called to, this battle for our family, the one we have, not the family we thought we had, will be won on our knees. Not in the court of current or public opinion, but in the secret place with Him where He shows us how to love and learn, that place where wisdom and mercy flow. He comes into the desert of our existence and plants roses along the way.

What have we believed? If we want a glimpse of this, look back on the narrative we have told our kids throughout their childhood. Dinnertime conversations. Unseen, unguarded moments. What are the words we have spoken concerning homosexuality? Our kids know what they have been raised with, the rhetoric, the slurs. Have we made growing up a safe space for them when they may have been grappling with "forbidden desire" for a long time? Table talk…life-changing, devastating, disparaging, or loving? What do we speak of when no one is looking? Because our littles have been onlookers for a long time! What jokes have we told in unguarded moments? Do we want to be deemed "right," or do we want to keep relationship with our child? I wonder if there are any places we need to ask forgiveness for, to repent to our kids as we clumsily press through to our new reality.

5

WHEN...

Take a breath! Stay calm! Let the person talk, for goodness' sake! Your mind might be going a million miles a minute...take another breath!

Consider the honor that your child has trusted you with, this very personal secret. They have let you into really deep places in their lives. Make notes, if that's what it takes to absorb what you are hearing, but LISTEN to their words and keep the door of communication open.

What we don't want to do is alienate our kid in what is a vulnerable and authentic moment in their life. We need to not treat our child any differently than we did before. In hearing long-distance through a Facebook message, I was nervous about the next time I'd see my kid, wondering, "Was he different? Had he changed? Would he look the same?"

When our child has trusted us, told us something that could change the whole dynamic of the way we relate as a family, it is an honor for them to bring us into the deepest secrets of their heart. We need to park any feelings of being blindsided. Maybe we were—it probably won't be the last time. Sideswiped or not, wherever we are in the line-up of information being dispensed, our child has told us something about themselves, and that is a privilege! Our kids are not an issue, nor a label. They are individuals who we have the privilege to love.

Embrace your child. Especially now, they need to be assured of your love. Please don't express it through pursed lips, but through tangible, felt love and care. Knee-jerk reactions, writing our child out of our lives or wills, acting out in our ambivalence, are not helpful.

Every person reading this will have a different story of how they "found out." We all find out in different ways. Wherever this realization will impact you, we must remember that our kid is still our kid, that bundle of love that we so eagerly welcomed into the world.

What is new to us has been well rehearsed by our child. Beware of reacting to their decisions in anger or haste. Remember, we the parent get to take the time we need too. We need to be ever mindful that we could be in danger of starting a chain reaction that we will never be able to reverse. Harsh words spoken will reverberate in hearts and minds long past the words escaping from our lips. We cannot retract edicts rashly spoken in the heat of anger and confusion. This is not a time to pop off at the mouth, but one to prayerfully walk with our Lord as we love and accept our child for the beautiful person God has created them to be.

Maybe we reacted, got angry, spewed verbal diarrhea. Unfiltered, unhelpful words spoken in haste slipped through our lips before we had a moment to think clearly. We cannot go back, but we can proceed from where we are at with humility, asking forgiveness where necessary. May we chase after the good of relationship rather than any false ideology—not always easy when the difference between what we believe and what we see playing out before us feels so wrong. What we are hearing flies in the face of our theology, we don't want to accept this new information, it feels too much at times...we have never been this way before, yet this son or daughter is the same one we taught to skip, to fish, to ride a bike. This is the one we labored with over spelling words or math problems. None of that has changed.

How can we move forward? Rob's elderly mother was dying of cancer when we told her about our son. We worried about how to tell Grammy! As a staunch Bible-believing Christian, how would she handle such new? My sister-in-law and I sat down for "the conversation" with her (we didn't want her to hear from someone else, and Rob was away on a mission). Grammy was disoriented with the news and couldn't quite figure out which son we were talking about (I have two boys). She was worried for my other son's children...shutting her eyes for a few moments, she said, "He needs a coat! It is winter," (he grew up in the islands of the Pacific and was about to face his first North American winter), "he needs a coat."

Grammy completely won me that day. She handled my kid's heart not with judgment, as her religious leanings might dictate. Instead, she took a pause, she listened to her God, and she chose to literally cover my son with her love. How thankful I am for a praying Grandma who saw us through many a trial with her fierce faith. Yay Grammy! She is looking on from heaven now, but I hope she knows she did good!

Yes, this is a story of the life of a family. It is not intended to be divisive, to make people mad. This is our journey with all its lumps and bumps, highs and lows. Maybe you are in that kind of journey yourself, wishing there was somewhere you could turn, some place for the answers you seek...grace, grace for this leg of the race as you figure out where you will land. This is not just a debate but the fight of our lives for the life of our family. When we land, may it be firmly on the side of love.

Remember, our child sharing their truth is a massive entrusting. They are taking a life-changing gamble on your response. To think that my boy basically had a contingency plan just in case we rejected him makes me shudder! Lord, that we would love well, and where we are clumsy, make quick amends.

It is OK for us to think and feel differently than our kids. We will. We do. But our goal is to come to a place where love covers, where we find what we agree on and go with that. If we operate on the basis that disagreement means division, we will be fractured and shattered. We are not whole if the places where we don't agree divide us. Surely our family means more to us on than the need to think and feel the same way! There are so many places we do not see eye to eye, is this the one that might cause us to throw our kids away? May it not be so! Our child walking away is one thing, us driving them away, that is another entirely.

We now have a new normal. This might not be what we wanted, asked for, or even expected, but here we are. If we need help to accept where we are at as a family, we would do well to seek outside counsel. Wise is the man or woman that does their own inner work in moving forward. On top of a new normal, we may not even be on the same page as our spouse. This too is confusing. Maybe there is disagreement between husband and wife as to how to handle things. Parents may be in very different places in their timeline of processing this new information that has been thrust upon their family. Mothers may want to take a very different route than fathers in their endeavor to love their child. Grace for this leg of the race. Space and grace to walk with Jesus in intimacy in this season of our lives. Mom, dad, grandparent, pastor, friend, concerned other, take time to do the work you need at the foot of the cross. This is not the time to tell the others processing alongside you that they are too soft, too lenient, too much.

Build a team. People who can be there for you, safe others you can express your anxieties and fears to about worries like HIV, grandchildren, etc. One friend expressed that when her child came out, she was terrified, afraid for her child's safety, the real threat of violence, bullying, and isolation. Pressures from without and within the gay world.

When I talked to my boy, he admitted there was a potential underbelly within the gay scene, things as a mother I don't even want to know about. Internal pressures, societal expectations are some of the sore realities to be faced as we pray.

Find a person who can help hold your heart as you navigate this new season. We have never been this way before. Consider talking to someone who has encountered the big questions you are currently facing. Even if you have never sought outside help in the past, if you are a deacon in the church, a pastor, counselor, a self-sufficient God-fearing person (if there is such a thing), get someone on Team You. You count too! Your needs also matter. Finding a safe landing place for our fears and anxieties relieves our child of the burden of taking care of us while they are trying to figure things out for themselves. We don't want to lay on them the millstone of fixing us, we don't want to alienate them in our relationship. As previously said, they've had a long time to think about where they are at, while we are playing a clumsy game of catch up. Peace for this portion of the chapter we find ourselves in.

A little after our son came out, we were on an anniversary vacation, where we met a new friend who became a daily coffee buddy. I will call him Keith. He graciously let us ask him questions about what he might have needed when he came out many years before. We so desperately wanted to do our best in loving our boy. What was helpful to Keith? What was destructive? We let him in on our journey, how we were wrestling with our new normal. Our early-morning coffee mate was so blessed when, after one of our conversations, Rob put his hand on his shoulder as he said goodbye. Rob's touch mattered to Keith. Even in a place where we looked at life very differently, Rob reached out from where he was at and conveyed warmth to the beautiful human that was Keith.

In a place where it feels there is so much to work out (especially if we are oral processors and need to verbalize), let us remember to look for areas that we can agree on as opposed to just argue about. Agreement not argument. God pursues our heart—how awesome is that? May we in turn pursue the heart of our child, not just their choices, but who they are, who God created them to be. May we literally reach out and touch one another heart and soul.

6

SAME SEX ATTRACTION

Same sex attraction is a real thing. Being attracted toward that which was created same. I am not sure I understood this. When my man came out as gay, I asked him if anyone had touched him when he was growing up. Our kids had the privilege of being raised while we were on a mission, and my husband and I were both very involved in our work. Could someone have violated my son? That was the first place I went as I asked some hard questions. You see, I had the faulty view that almost all homosexuality came out of an abusive situation (sorry about that!), rather than accepting the fact that feelings of same sex attraction had been a part of my child's thought process for a long time, this not being the result of predatory behavior on the part of another.

I have another friend, Beth, an incredible worship leader, who fell head over heels in love with someone of the same sex. We wrestled together, as only true friends can. In the end, where they landed was "This is the biggest gamble I have ever taken. Will God still love me if I go into this? If God is who I think He is, will He still love me?" Pray for the steadfast love of God to meet our kids where they are at, putting the right people in their path, those who represent His love, not an imitation.

Same sex attraction within the context of a local church is incredibly isolating. Our gay kids are lonely! Something is missing in the way we as communities of faith reach out to them, or in the way we don't reach out to them. A quick "Hi" from across the room just doesn't cut it. God has designed us all for relationship and intimacy. How many gay kids have we shown love to lately?

Beth is an amazing person with the call of God on her life. She wishes the church had been able to care for her differently in her in her situation. "Eloquent sermons are preached about it, we have our pat answers about grace, but how are we living it? We preach it and teach it, but for some reason, when it comes to homosexuality specifically, grace does not apply."

Grace can be life-changing! Beth says, "If I was shown that grace and mercy from people I respected and looked up to, I know in my soul that would have changed everything." How can we operate and show up differently for those we love?

Beth speaks of her same sex attraction as something she had been battling and suppressing for years. She was saved at fourteen, clearly has the call of God on her life, and was groomed for ministry accordingly. She says she "begged God to take away" the feelings she had. "I didn't want to be gay. I did everything I could to deny these urges." For a long time, she felt she had "control over it," throwing herself into God and doing His work "until temptation came," which was the time "I knew judgment would be harsh if I was to confess I was struggling."

In Beth's situation, she had seen people shamed and vilified when they were honest about where they were truly at. Rejection and alienation seemed to be the speedy, inevitable result of openly attempting to enter into a dialogue concerning same sex questions while searching for help, and all of this being with leaders she had trusted. On one occasion, she spoke up, seeking counsel in her search for understanding, and was given a "Band-Aid" prayer. We pray, we send people away...left to struggle alone. Isolation from community seems to be an answer we have employed. Beth says, "I saw the writing on the wall, and I knew I couldn't confess to my own struggles. I knew they would treat me like they had treated others before me. Fear gripped me." Shame kicked in, and she ended up "running and hiding" from church, a process that lasted many years.

Running from church had Beth running from her family. She had a secret. A secret life. When she was "outed," she wasn't ready. Afraid that the fear and rejection she was expecting would become her reality, she would have stayed in the shadows (a loss to the world, I might add). She talks about "not being able to live with myself."

How will we handle the Beths of our world? Will we sever the bonds we have built? Will we alienate, isolate, and reject? Thankfully, Beth's family was able, even if they didn't understand or agree, to grapple with their hearts and continue to love their girl. It paid off! It was an example of moms and dads doing their own work so they can continue in the work of loving their kids well.

Today Beth has a very "unique relationship with God outside the church walls." May the Beths of our world be driven toward Him, not away from His love.

7

OUR DILEMMA

Christians, we are in a dilemma! Where do we get our information? Who do we turn to when we are faced with some of the big questions of life? Do we just accept the rhetoric on either side of the argument as we fight for our family? We need to be aware of blind acceptance of what society believes versus what many of our churches might teach. Some of the schools of thought out there might tell us to throw our kids out, lock the door and dump the key, write them out of our wills, boycott their weddings! Our quest is an individual one. God saved us, loves us to freedom, and continues to walk with us in our human state. We have a chance here to walk the trails blazed by Christ, in His school, sitting at His feet every step of the way, seeking His answers for the questions of the moment. Is this something we will commit to do with Him, walking the pathways of Christ?

We don't want our thinking eroded by the world's

opinion, but formed by His Word, in His Presence. How is our prayer life for our child? Are we just wanting to argue with ideology, boycott what we don't understand? Imprecatory incantations are not what God wants from us. He has called us to love. Let our thinking be impacted by a daily, hourly, moment-by-moment relationship with Jesus, Who died to save us and wants the very best for us and our kids.

Just what should we believe? Peace as you journey! You may land somewhere different than us. We are not cookie-cutter Christians, we are those who have been called, and this journey for you is part of that call. Will we change our theology in the face of our current reality? In our experience, our convictions have not changed, but our compassion levels have.

Someone asked me if I felt my son's homosexuality disqualified me from ministry (don't you just love it?). My answer was, "No, it qualifies me all the more for all that He might call me into. God just widened my reach!" At a time when I was very busy in ministry, someone asked for an appointment. When I tried to get them to go to someone else, this request was met with, "It's a gay issue." My friend had watched the way we had loved our son and wanted to feel safe with those she let into her journey. May we be those people!

If you are a friend reading for friends, please be careful what you say! You are approaching those you genuinely care about in one of the most confusing times of their lives. This news is a game-changer for Christian parents, whether the world likes it or not. Narratives and scripts that have been believed and relied upon are all of a sudden up for trial. We all know Job's comforters…lovely creatures that they were…let's not be them! Let's be more!

A while after he came out to us, my son had a catastrophic accident where, as a pedestrian, he went under the wheels of a dump truck. It was a hit and run. A concerned Christian citizen asked me if I thought that the accident was some sort of divine judgement because of his lifestyle choices, possibly a retribution from God? Stunned, my only answer was, "Maybe your God, but not mine!"

Our words count! What we say has impact. Consider well the words you speak. Ask yourself, "If this was me, what would I need to hear?" Wonder along with your friends and be one who might be leaned on during the days ahead.

When we receive "the news," it may touch something in us. We need to be aware of what our own feelings are rather than transposing them onto our child. What's ours is ours, what's theirs is theirs. It's a "You deal with you, I'll deal with me" kind of thing.

There may be shock—indifference has no bearing within this discussion. Christian, if we are indifferent, we are not alive! Anger may be a factor. Grief. Questions. "What will my family end up looking like?" "Where do we go from here?" We have to deal with ourselves and our own reactions. What is getting stirred up in us? What exactly are we hearing as our son/daughter speaks to us of their sexual orientation?

Remember, Mama, Papa, you are a person too. You understand that it took courage for your kid to come out to you, but your feelings and thoughts are yours. You get to ask for space as you process if that is what you need. My son says it was a very long week after he wrote his note to come out and received my initial response of "I love you, son." I went "offline" for a week as I wrestled with my heart in the heart of God. We have needs in this equation too. I needed a minimum of seven days. What you need is not a weakness but part of the strength you will bring to the conversation as you all move forward, because like it or not, we are in this. This is our life, how will we choose to live it?

You don't have to react. You can ask for the space to process, to get with God and deal with it in the way that brings you most peace. Shalom for the path ahead. We are so often task oriented. We want to fix things, change things, make a plan, build solutions. Questioning how we can change our child is not helpful. Instead, invite your child to conversation, asking them, "How can I understand this from your perspective?" Invite dialogue rather than shutting them down. Asking how we can go forward in love is a good starting place.

Parent, it may be that we need to do some work of our own. Clearly, our children have been busy forming opinions, expressing desire. We have our own battles to face. If we don't do our own inner work, we will dump our junk in the lap of the next generation. What's ours is ours and cannot be answered by another. Where we struggle, consider wrestling this out with a trusted other, a mentor, counselor, pastor, friend. If we unburden ourselves onto our child without filtering years of deep feelings on this subject in this season, it can have catastrophic repercussions within our families. Fathers, particularly, might want to step in to fix or to help in any way they can. Answers, solutions, Band-Aids, Scriptures, proverbial "toolboxes" will be eagerly offered. Our child might not want our help, or at least not the help we want to offer. Our heart might be in a state of hemorrhage. We will bleed over those we love if we don't find a safe landing place for the legitimate questions and feelings of our own heart. Doing our own work helps us to come as whole as possible to the tables of discussion that might ensue.

Husbands may respond differently than wives. Beware of judging one another: "She's too soft," "He's too harsh." We need each other! This is not the time to point fingers but to give grace and space to navigate all that comes up in the moment. Flaws in our relationships may show up, historic happenings…where past bleeds into present and threatens to damage the future. We all need to do our own work. Get therapy or counsel, talk to true friends, assemble a team of trusted others around you that you might emerge from the shock of all that is going on as the most Christlike version of you possible.

Maybe we are dealing with feelings of shame. We can't believe this is happening to "our family." True community will be able to handle your life story without judgment. If there is shame because of a child's choice, questions beg to be asked: "What is going on in us? What does God have for us in this? As we do our own work, what is getting kicked up in us as we engage our current reality? If there is shame, where is it coming from? What is the deeper issue at play here?"

Where there is loss, we must grieve. Working through our expectations, what we wanted for our lives, how we saw the future playing out, how this interferes with our master plan, the picture in our mind—all these must be laid down at the cross where our healing and health comes from so that we can emerge more whole, able to engage the future with hope. Maybe we will be misunderstood, mislabeled, misrepresented for our stance of love, but it will be just a fraction of what our kids have faced, and if that doesn't rouse the Mama Bear in us, what will?

As we seek God in prayer, we ask, "What is true?" Beyond the stigma, what words of life does He have to speak over our family? Let us take this journey in faith. What will strengthen the relationship we have with our child? Are we willing to do the work of connection, even when it calls us to lean on Jesus instead of the dogma we have held so dear?

Do we want relationship with our children going forward, or do we just want them to conform to our image, the image we have created for them? May our prayer be, "Conform them to Your image, Lord," as we trust Him with every single detail that entails.

As praying people who find ourselves in a place of confusion and pain, one thing we can do is ask God for a word in this season. What is He saying to our hearts? How would He have us pray and cry out during this interval? This Lord Who knows the anguish of our hearts, the One Who never gives up on us, what does Jesus have to say? A word from Him makes all the difference every time! Are there Scriptures that He wants us to pray, to hold on to? Is there a word of life He is speaking that we can remind Him of? We get to enter this arena with a word from the Lord, one that will sustain us, keep us firm, an anchor for our faith in a hard place. Let us come with assurance that the God Who loves us so deeply has not abdicated the throne.

Ask Him for a hook for your faith: "What can I ask You for, Lord, in this situation, in this season?" He might surprise you with His answers, they might challenge you, change your thinking, but the intimacy with Him as you follow His words to your heart will be priceless. Oh, that we would take this journey into deeper connection with our Christ and our child.

We must never underestimate the power of God, His ability to move in our situations, whatever they be. If you have nothing else, start with the Lord's Prayer, "Thy will be done on earth as it is in heaven." Don't tell God what His will is, but submit before Him in this shock of your lives, surrender outcome and opinion into His loving hands, truly let God be God over all that you face. He is great, He is good, and He is well able to do exceedingly abundantly above and beyond all that you can ask or imagine. Let's not limit Him!

8

WHAT IS LOVE?

"What the world needs now is love sweet love..." We all know that song. And probably John 3:16 too: "For God so loved the world that He gave His only begotten son..." God's love gave and is a continually giving thing. Our love is often a taking thing. We love, we want more, we lust, we give in.

This is a weakened form of the Christian experience.

Some questions for us and our child might be around what love looks like. What does it look like for you? For me? It begs an answer. Is love something you take, something you give, or is it both giving and receiving? Is it mere sexual expression? What is love? Could it be bigger than the "what" we have confined it to be? Does the way we have typically loved need to expand as we continue this journey with our offspring?

As a parent, you might be grappling (and I hope you

are) with thoughts of "I don't want to lose my child!" We are desperate to maintain connection. What will it mean for us to love our child and not lose their hearts? Can we disagree and still maintain a loving, caring relationship? Wrapped up in this season of our sojourn may be a call from heaven to learn the enduring love of God in new ways.

Maybe our prayers are asking for every distorted illusion of love (ours and theirs) to be exposed, for smokescreens and fantasies of perfection be shown for what they are…true love can be hard work. Oh, that God would show what is real versus that which is false.

At. This point in our kid's journey, they have had many influences over their thinking. Where we land as individuals may factor into where our kids are at, but they have made big decisions about their sexuality, and we are frantically trying to get up to speed. What does it mean to love our kid and not embrace the whole gay megillah of the day?

We are challenged. Our beliefs have been called into question. We fear the potential loss of relationship if we don't agree with our kid. Some kids and some parents will take a "my way or the highway" attitude. Adult yourself into a place where you can love and accept your child where they are at and where you can parent your child into not reacting in the ways your younger self would have! It shouldn't be "my way or no way!" Take a breath, take a step back, and take time in His Presence to find His way forward for your family.

Some may ask, "What if he/she never changes?"

Friend, this is a faith journey, a call to pursue the heart of God and let Him fill in the blanks as we follow Him.

Fear is definitely a frequent response in this conversation. "Will we lose our child?" "Maybe my beliefs are wrong?" We fear the loss of relationship, both with our kid and our community, our church. We don't know how those around us will handle what is now our truth. What we have believed challenges our current reality, and we are just not yet sure where we will end up.

When our kid comes out to us, as we have already established, they know what we think on the subject. We raised them with our untested hyperbole. Our kids can quote us...our child knows that what they have revealed to the family has the power to divide or draw us closer together. Will they be accepted or condemned? Are we as parents going to default to "old school" thinking, or can we humbly believe that God is greater than the revelation of our child's sexual orientation and that heaven isn't having a panic attack because one of our children has very different thinking than we do? Can we love and be a safe landing place for our offspring, or do we want to drive them further into a life and lifestyle that is confusing and baffling to us and our Christian grid?

Even though we feel we are playing catch up, our son/daughter has done a lot of work to land where they have. We are a little late to the party. May we move with integrity, not telling God how this part of our story must play out. Can we commit not to fix or interfere but to persevere?

People ask me if "I knew." Man, that one is so loaded!

Knew what? That my son was kind and gentle and generous, that as the tallest person in the room I felt he should be have life skills that showed his sweetness and gentle nature? That being head and shoulders above his peers would make him an instant target for the wrath of every other toddler parent in the vicinity when peace was threatened? My son is a really fine human being, and no, I did not "know," I did not "suspect." I just loved my kid and am so thankful that it wasn't that complicated. You can be "nice" and gay/straight, you can be "mean" and gay/straight. We put so much pressure on one another in the course of living! Coming out is a deeply personal and life-altering moment for parent and child, something that our son/daughter has struggled and strained over, a revelation they are potentially prepared to alter the whole course of the family history with. My son believes it isn't the parent's issue (not sure I totally agree here). When they come out to us, it is an unfolding of their heart feelings. It's sharing a part of themselves with us, an entrusting. We run into problems when we, parent or child, demand "all or nothing"—"You completely accept me and my preferences, or **** you!" Surely love can be bigger than an ultimatum on either side of the chasm?

In life, we have to learn to live in the tension, the liminal places of almost and not quite, the wishes and the wants, the wonder and the woe. To live with the realities without rejecting those we love. May the gay reader also consider these factors. For either parent or child to decide "their way or no way" can add further difficulty to relationships as we fight for what is good going forward.

What might your offspring need from you? What might you need from them? These are good questions/life skills we might benefit from while we navigate where we are at as we press forward in love. Maybe this could be a new family dialogue: "We see things differently, but how can we walk together in love going forward?"

9

REAL VS. FAKE

Some years ago, a friend gave me a mug, a lovely mug made by a Canadian artist. The beautiful design and delicate china have given me much joy over the years, and I still enjoy drinking my tea from it. On one of my forays into the world of retail pleasure, I was in a bargain store and spied the very same mug—though it was not the same. It looked the same, seemed to be the same quality, had the same design, but one was real and the other was fake. Nowadays, I can hardly tell them apart unless I look underneath at the inscription.

Are we like this in life? Parent/child, have we have accepted something that is not real? A version of the truth that looks so close to the original that we are confused as to which one is real and where we should really land in our thinking? My "real fake" looks the same, feels the same, but one is the true work of the master, the other is a copy made as a look-alike.

My prayer is that we will chase after the true and not get confused along the way. That we will all be rightly attached to the love of God, our hearts landing in an authentic place. Let us not be mistaken—there is much work to do! May we not settle for being so close to the real thing that we miss that which is the true. I write this to both us and our beloved offspring.

Ephesus, Turkey, is one of my favorite places to visit. On the outskirts of the ancient city, there is a guy who sells watches. His sign reads "genuine real fake." I love this sign and the lesson to my heart!

Let us not be people of the genuine real fakes but press in to the truth. Because I "feel" something does not make the feeling real but just a feeling that might pass, something that comes and goes. What we are feeling right now in our journeys is quite likely to change, especially if submitted into the hands of a loving God. Let us not limit ourselves or lock ourselves into one way of thinking or acting over another.

May we deepen in our experience of God, crying out to Him for that which is genuine, that which originated in His Heart for us. Then, we won't cling to fake love, false expressions, imperfect parenting, the genuine fake of our experience.

May God broaden, expand, enlarge, and grow us into the *Imago Dei* that He intends for us to reflect. Let us not settle, remembering that He defines right from wrong—that is not our job. And while our son or daughter works on their testimony, may we entrust them to the hands of the One Who loves them perfectly to lead and guide them on their way.

Is it possible that sometimes we are called to press through difficult places so that others might take comfort when they journey along similar pathways as they seek to make sense of where they are at?

If we think this will one day go away, we are mistaken! Regardless of where we land in our thinking, people who hold a traditional biblical view and people who differ in their expressions will continue to be at odds with one another. Finding true balance may be a pendulum, swinging from point to point, a moving target. We might never agree, continuing to be diametrically opposed to our parents/children, but agreement might not be the goal here.

Higher than a desire to agree is the power of love, where we can love and want the best for the other, even if we do not subscribe to the course taken. Open dialogue and communication, devoid of judgment and condemnation, might be our higher aim. To walk in love, making space for differing opinions, even if we never land on the same page. Can we love?

So then, the question begs to be answered: What do we believe about God and His love? What does God's love look like to you? Is God some fickle being who zaps His subjects when they err? Is the love of God big enough to handle our hearts as we pursue a place of peace in loving our same sex attracted child? Can God handle the sexual feelings our kids have toward someone of the same gender?

What do we believe about God and His love? Can we live in the tension of our circumstances being as they are and not try to have our theology accommodate our reality? Not changing things up to fit our reality, but coming afresh to the Father, asking for His heart as we journey forward.

At the end of the day, it is not the "haters" who will stand before Jesus and answer for the way we loved our kids, even if their opinions are loud! We will give account for our own lives, how we acted, reached out, extended ourselves to those He gave us and to the LGBTQ community in general. What conviction is He calling us into as we ponder these things? How will He find the intentions of our heart?

What is God asking of us as we navigate these deeper questions? What does God want of us? How do we love well as we walk with our child? May He find us faithful!

Is it as simple as blind acceptance versus total judgment? Is there space for "I can't agree with you, but can we keep the love lines open?"

In looking at how others have weathered the same sex attraction storm that might have hit their family, it is easy to make judgments, to form opinions on the behavior or intentions of others. This is part of the message of parenting a child of the rainbow, that we not judge how others handle where they are at, that we not judge our child, that our child not judge us...we might be flying blind here, and if not, we may feel like we are flying solo.

Whichever way things end up has a lot to say about the strength of relationship we have with our child, and if we don't like where we have found ourselves, there is still time to repair things. In fact, it is imperative we do all we can to walk in love with one another. Can we agree to disagree, holding mutual regard and affection for each other?

There was a time in our marriage when I spoke up about something to my husband. When I was offended that he didn't "listen" to me, his response was, "just because I have listened to you does not mean I will do what you are asking of me or that I agree with you." We may never land where our kids are at, and vice versa, but can we err on the side of love and let God work out all the details?

"When you pray…" Sometimes we pray in faith, and sometimes we pray in hope. As we pray, may He till the soil of our soul. When my boy was comatose, crushed and left for dead after the hit and run I mentioned, I asked the Lord, "What can I ask for, what may I pray for today?" I meant it. I had no idea how to pray effectively in that situation. I was desperate. Knowing that I didn't want to ask amiss, I asked how: "How shall I pray today, Lord? What can I ask for today?"

One day it was asking for breath, one day for the "bones that had been broken" to rejoice, one day it was "women who had received their children as back from the dead"—why couldn't I be one of those? God is creative with the ways He might have us pray, but remember, His prayers always get answered.

Today my son, my amazing gay son, is vibrant living proof of answered prayer, of the fact that our merciful God sees, hears, and knows what we have need of. He is not oblivious to your plight at this time. Ask for the Word of the Lord, for the prayer of the Spirit in your unique situation.

What is it that Father wants to reveal to your heart as He hovers over the deep things you are going through? Pray with Him, not just to Him, praying in synchrony with Holy Spirit. Let the stories He is writing in heaven come to pass here on earth.

10

MINE VS. YOURS

What's mine is mine, what's yours is yours... we each have to carry our own load. Bear one another's burdens, but carry our own load. When a child comes out to their family, all sorts of flaws might emerge in the basic structure of the home and the health of the relationships. We have to do our own work. We cannot blame the dog, our child, the preacher, our wife, or our husband. We must do the deep work in our own hearts. This might be a lifetime journey, and the grief we feel will perpetuate greater pain if we don't find the peace we need as we progress.

We did some ministry in Africa, and one of our friends there said, "I leave you in peace, not pieces." May we find peace in the midst of the pieces! What will you do with the losses you bear? How will you handle your feelings of bereavement as you handle your child's choices? We often want the Cliff notes, to take the test without doing the deeper work, wanting to circumvent the process. Let us not short-circuit the Spirit of the living God and the deeper work He invites us into with Him.

Will we be those who bring our feelings of bewilderment to God, sitting at His feet, waiting for His love to flood our hearts? Jesus, the One Who chose not to cast a stone when He could, He's the person we need to sit with, looking at what He sees, learning what He knows, loving as He loves. Communing with Him, asking what He has for us in the places we are at, the circumstances we are in, He speaks into our situations with His truth, His love, His peace.

Recognizing that His ways are higher than ours, that He might have different priorities than we do, we have our own journeys to take. We can't walk for another. What's mine is mine, what belongs to my child is theirs. We need to give space for a deeper work within both us and our progeny as we live in this fallen world. May our story reflect His glory, that what currently feels like a total heartache may be the birthplace of fresh hope. Whatever our narrative has been till this point, are we willing to explore the path of a deeper love?

God is sovereign, He created us, man and woman. He gets us where we don't get ourselves, and He will meet us in the places we are at. Never underestimate the power of God to come through in the most unexpected of ways!

Not everything we have believed is necessarily true, and this goes for all angles or aspects of any equation. We have to ask ourselves, "What is He asking of me? What does He require of me in this season?" Even if it be costly, will we set aside what we think we know in pursuit of knowing Him, learning His kingdom, not the version we have created for ourselves, His new way of doing and being in this world?

Mother, father, son, daughter, how do you handle desire? Sexual expression is not always a cure. Sometimes it is part of a pattern that is not ultimately helpful. We tend to stave off our feelings of need and insecurity, thinking sex will fix them—it does not. Acting out in any relationship will not heal us, and it could hinder our growth before God and one another. Are we at peace, or are we using sex as a Band-Aid to cover a multitude of woes? Are these questions we could ask our kids (after we have done our own work, of course)?

What drives our need? Have we ever acted out of a deep-seated sense of loneliness? Our gay kids often are desperately lonely! They are sometimes the "untouchables" in church culture, even in churches where the preaching is impeccable and the worship fantastic. Friends, gay kids are lonely in the church. What can we do about this? Are we as a body of believers driving kids deeper into the gay community because our fellowship is exclusive, unaware, suspicious of those with same sex attraction? Gay kids who love Jesus often feel they don't fit into the things we hold so dear, or if they fit, it can only be within the lines that have been drawn in the tenets that are held by leadership. I don't say this in judgment. We have much to examine as people of faith, loving every individual and leading the way to Jesus and His love. We don't understand, but will we believe God, the God Who "so loved the world, He gave"? He always lands in love, and He knows how to communicate truth to us and our kids. Let us not limit God and His power to work and accomplish the things that concern us.

When faced with big things, I ask for little things along the way to pray for. When my son was on life support, I prayed for the next breath, then the next. As each prayer was answered, faith grew. How are we praying for our children, gay, trans, queer, straight, bi, non-binary, whatever label they might prefer? What prayers of faith—not judgment or condemnation—are we praying for them? That none of our kids get lost in the weeds of what the world has to offer, that they land in His hands, the hands that took the blows of the hammer, the agonies of the cross? He knows how to rightly love our kids toward the Father.

As I write, it occurs to me that I don't have much to say about behavior, but lots about right connection with the Trinity. This is how I pray for my kids, all of them, whether married, single, straight, or gay: "Lord, let them be rightly connected to You, into intimacy with Your Presence, friendship, love, and unbroken fellowship." Praying this for ourselves, for anyone, is transformative. If we are rightly related to Him, it will change everything about and around us.

When a child is born to our home, we have hopes and dreams for that person. Each child is a gift and a treasure. Some of us may have to grapple with unmet expectations, hopes deferred, disappointment. Our kids face the same internal battles…when they come out to us, they don't know how we will handle it. There are so many unknowns, we find ourselves in foreign territory. Our faith is challenged, our traditional beliefs are called into question. What we believed, are those things still true? Where do we think we now fit in the world as we knew it? One thing my son genuinely cared about was how his coming out would affect our ministry: Would our mission agency reject us? (They did not.) Ethan realized his choices would impact our world.

What's ours to carry is ours, and we cannot expect others to pick up the fragments of our thinking. If our belief system is shattered, we go to the Author and Finisher of our faith, land there, and He will walk with us through every detail.

When a child comes out, they may be an adult, an adult who has the charge to work out their own salvation with fear and trembling. What's theirs is theirs, not mine. We all do our own work, not the work of another. Is the God we serve big enough for the situation we find ourselves in? If not, we need to plug in for an upgrade of hope in His Presence.

Are we looking to our child for something that is not theirs to give us? Is our heart overly wrapped up in our kid's accomplishments? Are we "good proud" or sinfully pride-ridden that homosexuality is robbing us of bragging rights among our friends? Is there twisted thinking in us that needs a trip to the cross where we are cleansed? We get it so wrong, and when we do, we cease to be authentic followers of Christ in this area. Maybe our tendency is to want to hide parts of ourselves and our experience.

Someone said, "What is hidden cannot be healed." May we allow the Spirit to shine His light as we unapologetically seek God for the very best He has for our child's life, remembering that the Holy Spirit has a specific journey for us and a plan for our offspring. May His plans come to pass.

11

THE CHURCH

So often we make our conversations about behavior when Jesus often did not. When looking at Zacchaeus or the woman caught in adultery (I often wonder where the man was in this story!), Jesus didn't address lifestyle. He said to Zacchaeus (in Allison's own version), "Hey, man—I'm coming to your house!" (Luke 19:5). Jesus didn't deal with behavior, He addressed connection. Let us connect! We cannot behave our way into the kingdom. We have to encounter Christ and let Him figure out the details as they come up. We might never land where our kids are in this topic, as has already been stated, but landing on the same page isn't the point. Our call is to "owe no man anything except to love one another" (Romans 13:8).

Where has the church missed it or dropped the ball? Have we been afraid to engage in the conversation? Have we been so absorbed in debating ways of behaving that we have lost our voice, the sounds of His love? If so, we need to find our way back to the heart of the Father.

Historically, we have tended to weaponize Scripture or eject the offender. We may have shaken our heads when we have heard it said that the church is the only agency that shoots its own wounded, but we have then gone on to participate in such a scenario. How has this worked for us? Where are we lame and crippled, where have we been wounded by words or had the Word used as a weapon against us? Where have we been the perpetrator in such practices? What we have done has weakened and wounded when we are called to bring life and speak it forth.

May God give us the mind of Christ as we engage in the LGBTQ+ conversation. Prayerfully, we can invite Jesus into our thought processes, asking that wherever we differ from Calvary love, He would show up and give revelation and that we would align our thoughts with His. And in places we do not think like Jesus, that He would correct us and bring us into greater congruence with His love that gives.

Buckle up, my friends! We have been given a divine entrusting to do the love of God differently than typical Christian culture says we should. This is the stuff moves of God are made of!

In our desire to follow biblical order, we are called to surrender the values we come in with in deference to His, knowing that many of us believe differently today about certain things than when we first knew Christ. Even if we have perfect theology, maybe our love button needs recalibrating. We may need to let go of our ideals and pet peeves in surrender to His heart, to submit our wishes, preferences, and dreams to the love of Christ, asking, "Where can we grow in this journey of loving our kids with all that we have?" Are we willing to wait on God as we wait alongside our offspring, even if things don't look like we wish they would? Can we hang out in the mess while the message is being formed? My son is working on his testimony, and so am I...

> *But as it is written:*
> *"Eye has not seen, nor ear heard,*
> *Nor have entered into the heart of man*
> *The things which God has prepared for those who love Him"*
>
> — 1 CORINTHIANS 2:9

Our stories are not over yet, they are still being written, and like the old-school preachers used to say, "We've read the back of the book, and the outcome is good!" We must never underestimate the power of God to move in the most amazing of ways in the lives of His people.

The church has typically been afraid to talk about sex, any sex. We have been timid on the topic of rape, abuse, incest, and homosexuality, sometimes unwittingly or ignorantly allowing it to continue in our midst because we couldn't conceive that "our people" would be involved in such things. We have protected perpetrators and silenced victims. Often the church has had a "just say no" policy, believing that if we just said, "Don't do it," that would magically deliver us from the evils going on in our congregations. Representatives from houses of worship have recoiled in disgust when people have turned to them for advice and understanding. Such a lack of compassion! We have blamed the victim, called them liars, not believing them or acknowledging the pain they were in. Sexual sin and abuse have been hidden within the bowels of our institutions by clumsy attempts to present ourselves as righteous, all the while discounting the voices of those who tried to speak up. Not our finest hour. We have run from things we felt would rock the boat.

Pastor, parent, what we need is a bigger conversation! The world celebrates "If it feels good, do it," but this is not biblical. There are consequences to everything we do. Complete license is not the answer either!

We can't just be poking around in the Word to protect our pet peeves. The Bible is our authority—may our thoughts and attitudes come into line with His.

There are gay kids in our congregations. They are tired. They know the rhetoric. Purity is something we hold dear. Have we taught a gospel of "being good"? A canon of "you can't"? A dogma of "don't!?" We train people to "be good," but has it cost us? Has it cost us a generation of people who struggle and have found compassion and care to be lacking in the church? Have our ways of missing the mark caused others to move away from community, something to which we are all called?

Let us not be fooled: Sex is an intoxicating force, something that we are drawn to. We have given it a power it doesn't really have, while at the same time denying the force it actually has. Worldly thought says it will take away all of our problems, all the while those that stand to minister on a Sunday often steer very clear of the subject. Is it any wonder that our kids are going elsewhere for the answers they need?

Under the microscope of conflicting opinion, will we keep loving even when we might think and feel so differently from one another?

When we planted a church among a population coming out of addiction, we built in a smoke break before taking the offering. This wasn't to make the people more generous, it was to be with them where they were at until, for some of them, smoking was no longer an issue. Many of those fine folk have gone on to serve God and change their worlds, their destinies. Very few held on to smoking, but tobacco wasn't really the issue. The matter in question was loving our people to the foot of the cross, the place where God's finest work is done, and we don't get to dictate the what, how, or when of it. Redemption is God's work, not ours. We just get to love along the way.

Notwithstanding the struggles, can we offer to adventure together, entering the world of another? Instead of rejection and isolation, can we create safe spaces where we can hear what is being said without judgment or laying down the law? Are we being called back to the revolutionary love of Jesus? Is it possible that, as a result of our abdication of relevant presence in culture, we have left the media, MTV, or a certain family whose name begins with K to pick up the slack concerning how we live in this world?

How then shall we respond? What is His call to us in this season? Blindly believe the verbiage of one side or another, or find a new way through the maze, a way that leads to Jesus and His love?

Churches may be in the position to minister to child and parent alike. Pushy tactics will not work. An ultimatum is not the answer, neither is another Bible study. Parents need a safe landing place with their shock and grief, somewhere to go with the pain they are experiencing. Hurting parents do not need to be chastised for where they went wrong or their child's choices. In the same vein, their children want to be valued members of the church, not just tolerated or seen as the lepers of the house. God help us that we don't hold back affection and love from anyone, regardless of their sexuality. My son talks of a "rainbow ceiling" in the church, much like the glass ceiling many have experienced. What does this mean to us as we follow Jesus in our own setting? As we look not to license but to love?

When we first began to attend our current church home, I chatted to the pastor, asking him if he really believed in the love he so eloquently spoke from the pulpit, if the words from the front were a true reflection of the heart of the house. In our search for a place to land in the Spirit, we wanted to know that our kid would be safe where God had called us to be. One parent said, "Maybe we shouldn't take our kids to a church that has a lot of older members as they might be more judgmental." Elder saints, can we be the love of Jesus free of judgment in a hurting world? As parents grapple deeply with all the personal feelings that are coming up, will we as their community of faith have the grace to embrace their gay kids just as they are? Can we look them in the eye, enjoy them, authentically engage them, or will we drive them further away from the precious love of God and His people?

Many years ago, I was in Bible study, and we were jammed in pretty tight with five people on the couch as we studied the word of God. I was in the middle, with someone on my right and left. During the course of the study, I distinctly heard the voice of the devil (imagine a creepy voice) saying, "She's gay." These words barely had the chance to hit home when the Holy Spirit countered, "You stay right where you are!" It was an imperative from heaven, a life-altering edict. "Do not move, do not extract yourself from contact...This is my child, who I love." Precious gay reader, forgive me that this was my truth. We all have a long way to go as we examine outdated prejudices that may have been passed down through family lines.

As a church, we had to be willing to be seen by other people of religious persuasion as the "gay church." Would we be a place of welcome for all, where any could come and worship as God works out the details of our salvation? May God help us all to align our hearts with Him and His love for the whole of mankind.

Could we be willing to partner with the timeline of the Holy Spirit, that we not run ahead of God and His timing but give space for Spirit? God can and will attend to the intricate details of all of our lives when, where, and how

He wants to. We can unite with the Trinity as He actively tends to all of our souls. His timing, not ours.

May we commit to the adventure of conversation with those we disagree with sans judgment. Pre-formed opinion and prejudice have long reigned in our thinking. It is time we had an encounter with the living God where we wage war for the hearts and souls of people, not their behavior alone.

Cultures are clashing in this great debate: Our culture, our child's culture, and His culture. We have to be very careful as we pass sentence concerning things that puzzle us. Not a one of us has everything figured out in intimate detail. Mercy triumphs over judgment, and I would rather land in mercy than take the role of judge in matters where I am still a student or a curious one myself. God defines right from wrong, not me, and He has ways beyond ours to work out the details of our lives.

Sometimes we try and fight the wrong battles. Realizing that there are certain things God hates but that He loves people, is it not enough for our prayer to be "Lord, let my child know You in the deepest places of their heart," asking for them and us to be rightly attached to Jesus, that we grow in the mind of Christ, that anything that has power over us—all of us—will be surrendered in relationship with Him? Sin takes something God intended for good and uses it in ways different than God's design.

Struggle is part of the human condition. I have my issues, you have yours. Who gets to decide who has the greater sin/struggle pattern and when God will meet with us as we walk with Him? For my son, in my prayers I ask for him to be in right relationship with Jesus (I ask this for all five of my kids). Everything else is a detail for the God of the universe to take care of. May we love without compromise and not compromise because of love.

If you have ever ridden the Tube in London, you will have heard the phrase "Mind the gap." There is tension in the gap. It is in the in-between places that we must be aware lest we fall. Some of the gaps are pretty big, liminal spaces in our lives, the gaps between what we believe and the realities we live with. Mind the gap, my friends. May God fill the gaps with His Presence and peace in our hearts.

We all have biases. Gay and straight alike, we hold negative and positive bias. Preston Sprinkle says in his book *People to be Loved*, "Don't trade a day of being right for a lifetime of influence." May we hold space in the Spirit for truth to be revealed to our hearts. God speaks, especially when we take the time to wait for Him to invade our earthy experience with His heavenly one. Heaven on earth, come!

12

LIFE GOES ON

Human nature is always looking for the easy answer. We want the way of least resistance, the path of lesser suffering. Possibly our child thought that when they came out, some of their troubles would be over. Now they can live without the lie they have been sheltering under, the secret that threatened to topple the family with its potential to destroy their relationship with their parents and siblings. Now they can come out of hiding.

Thus far, their journey has been paved with scary possibilities, some of which have been realized. Coming out for your child will not end all their problems, or yours, it will just reposition them. Where there is narcissism, in them or us, it will crave an audience. Fear, anger, unresolved pain, anxiety, pride—these will all remain, sometimes out of sight, but they will be there awaiting an opportune moment for the weeds to emerge.

We all have to work on our own stuff. "You do you" is a phrase we might have used. We have to do us and the work that being us involves. Each of us must do our own heartbreaking labor, that which is ours. I cannot do my son's work, he cannot do mine. Sometimes we are so focused on the work another needs to do that we neglect that which belongs to us. Are the weeds of judgment, religion, or prejudice being harbored instead of respect, compassion, and tenderness? Remember, coming out as gay is not going to solve all of life's problems. It may create a few difficulties that were totally unforeseen!

> *"Love is large and incredibly patient. Love is gentle and consistently kind to all...love does not traffic in shame and disrespect, nor selfishly seek its own honor. Love is not easily irritated (overly sensitive) or quick to take offense...love is a safe place of shelter, for it never stops believing the best for others...love never gives up"*
>
> — 1 CORINTHIANS 13:4–7 TPT

To this we are called, accompanying Christ in the journey of love, the life-laying-down, cross-carrying adventure He has brought us into. The labors of love, the hard work of His affection for us, that which caused Him to hold nothing back, no price too high, the brutal cost of His passion for relationship, the pathways of pain for the prize of our hearts...how far will we go for the heart of our child? For this dear one you so lovingly nurtured and cherished in their journey thus far? Hard conversations may need to be had, but let us never lose sight of the call to love. May the love of Christ be our bottom line. Not that which we have assigned to the Trinity, nor that which we have typically believed, but that which He wants to breathe into us in this season as we walk this path leaning on our Beloved.

Could this be a time to re-evaluate thoughts old and new, long-held belief systems that might not be applicable in this earth-shattering time? What has worked in theory may not hold up in reality. For us, this is earth shattering! We are searching for answers, trying to make sense of things that seem to be happening around us. Lots of things we thought we knew about our family, it seems, are not true. Our kid, that one we cherished, raised to think like us, has a mind and will of his/her own...things are not what we imagined. Wondering at times which way is up, let us look higher, to Him Who loves us more and wants the best for all of our lives. May we know peace that passes understanding, even in the storm. May we rest in the settling power of His love.

We have not been abandoned in this. As I have mentioned, it would be easier if we could blame our kids, our grandparents, ourselves, our God, or the dog! We may even have looked for someone else to be culpable for our kid's choices. Someone should pay... Friend, someone did! Jesus took the agonies of this life. He paid full price, whatever it took, the total cost, all so we could know our Father. May we calm our hearts in the work God has done to rescue us where we needed it, to straighten (no pun intended) us out or up, to iron out the wrinkles of our complicated hearts. In this spirit of being so deeply loved by God, we can come with gratitude as we pray.

Seismic shifts occur when we tackle these things in the context of family. Walking through homosexuality can expose flaws that might have been latent, waiting for an outlet (this is true for any potential stressor in the family system). As parents, we need to commit to pulling together, not falling apart—choosing a path of mutual respect, listening to one another as a couple, finding a place of compatibility that is as close to or congruent with one another as possible. Allowing mutual respect to flourish. The latter can be tricky if the parents are diametrically opposed in their thoughts. If we find ourselves at odds with one another in defense of our kids, we must find something we can agree on, working with our current reality. This is not the time for a civil war! Remember, we are on the same team. Let's do the work of pulling together so we don't fall apart.

At the end of the day, we cannot make choices for our adult child. If we are invited, we can advise and give input, but our autonomous adult offspring has the same free will we have been granted, and they will use said gift, hopefully with wisdom!

May our words be "seasoned with salt," that which preserves and adds flavor as we endeavor in love one with another. How can we be gracious as we care for the heart and soul of families who are grappling with something as challenging as homosexuality? Maybe you are reading this for someone else, a friend, a loved one. How can we extend the love of Christ in a situation where people are hurting?

We often play an unintended role in pushing our kids further from God's love. Are we willing to extend the love of Christ, or will we drive our child closer to the things that we don't agree with by our being vehemently opposed to where they are at as people? If you are reading this and have stuck with me thus far, I imagine you want to draw your child near, not drive them from the good of what your family system might have to offer. People tend to gravitate to where they are loved, where they are more than endured. What can we celebrate with our family member, not just tolerate?

God has been good in our kids' lives. Let's remember those things as we rehearse His mercy and His love. Speaking truth, may we not weaponize the Word of God as we relate to one another. We are entering into a long-term love. A long term of loving. Sometimes the Spirit does not work on our schedule, but remember, He takes His orders as a part of the Trinity and is never late! What about when the Spirit seems slower than we want Him to be? Are we willing to surrender outcome to Him who knows every intimate detail of our lives. Are we waiting to see God show up as only He can, working out the minutiae to His intricate perfection?

Will we take time to listen to His voice over the noise around us, tuning in to the sounds of the Spirit and letting the cacophony of philosophy and ideology we are confronted with come into perspective? In the throne room of the Almighty, what is the most important thing? What really matters as I come toward Jesus and His love? As I attend to Him and His Presence, that which seems so big has a way of being filtered, clarified, reclassified. Wherever we are at in our journey, may it draw us into that secret place with Him where the angst and the agony, the anger, and deep feelings can melt away in the mysteries of His great love, finding His peace for our process, all the while holding onto and remembering that this season is a sacred entrusting from Him. We get to walk with our kids through the maze that is ahead. May we walk well, my friends.

13

WHAT ABOUT THE WEDDING?

Weddings! Marriage, that holy institution designed to reflect God's love and care for mankind. If we have thoughts about homosexuality, we also have thoughts about what we would do if... Would we attend the wedding of a same sex attracted child to a person of the same gender?

Individual choice is once again at play here. Mothers and fathers may be in very different places concerning the wedding of a same sex attracted child. Some questions to ask ourselves are: "Would we go to the wedding of a heterosexual couple who have been living together?" "Would I attend the wedding of a couple pregnant out of wedlock?" "Shall I attend the nuptials of my divorced child?" "Will I irreparably damage my relationship with my child if I don't go to his/her wedding?"

Are we able to agree not to agree with a child's philosophy but still move forward in loving relationship? How might we prepare our hearts and minds as we ponder our gay kids and their desires for marriage and family?

A very painful moment for us, for both parents and child, was when our son asked my husband if he, as a pastor, would marry him when he eventually meets his special someone. Think about that one for a moment. Rob paused and said, "I can't, Son. I will celebrate you, but I can't marry you." Hard moments like this might come up. Big questions that beg answers.

Love can be hard work sometimes! Being there for our kids can fly in the face of our flesh, as every parent who has responded to a 3 a.m. wake-up call knows. This is the work of love. It doesn't always fit the boxes we have built to contain it.

Other tensions may arise, such as "If you don't love this about me, you don't love all of me." On some things we may differ. Unconditional love is a gift regardless. Love isn't about loving everything, it is about loving through everything. Life is messy, and we don't like every aspect of this call to love. Love anyway, for to such are we commissioned.

"What about the boyfriend/girlfriend?" Will we extend the same affection to a partner of a same sex couple that we would in our other children's relationships? Early on, I decided that if someone was going to be in my son's life, I wanted them in mine. This turned out to be a true gift! When my son was out on a date while in college, a dump truck turning right on red took out my son, a pedestrian who had the right of way. He went right under the wheels of that truck, which just drove on. The boyfriend my son pushed out of the way, the guy I had just that week made my Facebook friend, was able to contact me and tell me the terrible story of that night. That one thing might have saved my son's life in that I was able to speak to medical personnel. I am grateful that guy was in my life, grateful to have had an open line of communication with the boyfriend of my son. Hopefully your story will never be quite as dramatic or life threatening as ours, but it's something to consider as we move forward in relationship. Maybe the question we should be asking is not what it will cost me to have a relationship with the love of my child's life but what it could cost if I choose not to.

We have to realize that our views about sexuality, cohabitation, and marriage may differ, as do our views about politics, climate change, recycling, and world peace. We may not agree on everything, but can we reach a decision to love? Can we engage an equal lens on the scope of love? Can we concur that the person in question will always be our child and we will never reject them? Are there inequities in the ways we love one kid over another?

The trigger has been pulled, and the gun is loaded. The prisms of our paradigm require us to clarify exactly what we believe. Why do we believe the things we do? Because we heard it preached? Because our grannies or grandads said so? Questioning accepted hyperbole may lead to fresh understanding.

Are we willing to excuse the porn, excessive obsession with the cell phone, work addiction, or gluttony in a person's life because it is easier to hide or manage versus the ways we try to cover up or minimize the reality of homosexuality that is staring us in face because we have been conditioned to attribute shame to such things? How much of our reaction to the homosexual debate is man driven because someone else spoon-fed us their philosophy, shaping our mindset, rather than it being modeled after the life of Christ and His love for mankind?

Can we ask for mutual patience as we struggle with opposing views, as we seek God for His definition of love in the day and age we live in? Can we bow down to God, not bend into the folklore of man? Respect for other as well as self is an imperative as we move forward.

As we pray, we can ask that anything that doesn't look like love be broken off. Love is not possessive, it does not consume, own, demand, or cannibalize. Love is patient and kind. If we are embroiled in anything that doesn't look like love, may it be surrendered for what is better. Many years ago, a catchphrase was "the good is the enemy of the best." This is a prayer of my heart for all five of my children, that they will never settle, never just go for the good but always wait for the best He has for them.

James K. A. Smith says in his book *You Are What You Love*, "We are oriented by our longings, directed by our desires." May we and our kids long for God, returning to our first love, if necessary, longing for God above all, that the love of God would be our orientation and that He would direct our desires.

This is a new day in the life of our family. Things may never look the same. Fresh ground has been broken whether we like it or not. Maybe we want to struggle with our child when that isn't where the real battle is. "We wrestle not against flesh and blood" (Ephesians 6:12). If we wrestle against flesh and blood, we will have a bloody mess on our hands in the literal sense of the word. How will He have us pray for our child in this new season?

A friend whose son is in a same sex marriage sagely said, "Live with no regrets! When it comes to weddings and family celebrations, don't tend to the feelings of people who aren't walking in your shoes. Attend to the heart of your child. You may have mixed emotions about the occasion. This is legitimate, but take the time to enjoy your grown child. Don't get bogged down with whether you will share pictures, and if you do, whether you will dare to smile or if you will worry about what people will say. We can be so worried about people's opinions that we don't even act like ourselves." Do we want to be "right," or do we want the right to stand with our kids through thick and thin, whatever life brings their way?

When it comes to the wedding, remember that our kids know how we think and feel. May we live well. My friend regrets that she was worried about others and how they might respond to their situation, and in some ways, it hindered her ability to really show up for her child. Her advice was "live with no regrets," this from a lady who has lived it, not from an onlooker or concerned other. Enjoy your child.

Like you, I have wondered about these questions: "Will I post pictures?" I would if this was an occasion for any of my other kids. "What will people say?" We all run our own race. Grace for yours as I navigate mine. Friend, religion has damaged and wounded so many, may it have no play here in this privilege we have of loving our kids. We have given the opinion of others power over us. Inordinate power. Let's take that back as we press through in loving our gay kids well. Everyone will have an opinion, surely, but we must bring our questions to the foot of the cross, letting Him shape and form our actions and reactions, his opinion being the one that we will allow to shape the direction we take.

Heart work must be done so we can be there for our kids in Christ-centered ways. Remember, our children know how we feel. Our theological viewpoint is known to them, they have lived with us, heard our stance on the issues of life, they are not a stranger to the ways we think. What messages have we poured into our kids over the years that, if given a "do over," we might approach differently?

How might Father be wanting to soften our heart as we continue to care for and love our child?

14

FURTHER THOUGHTS

Love is our bottom line. Love sometimes looks different than we want it to. It often takes longer than we are comfortable with. John 15:12 exhorts us to "love one another as I have loved you." Ponder a moment the love of God. How have we been loved? Has He been present to us even when we saw things differently than Him? What has the love of God looked like in our own lives? How can we extend that love to our sons and daughters wherever they land in the spectrum of life? I am so grateful for the patient love of God!

We have tried to explain away the gay, to argue it away, to reject, get angry, give tearful appeals and Bible tirades, all to no avail. Here we are, our lives not turning out like we thought they would…how will we best glorify God in this season? How will we extend His hand of healing in the nations, in our nation, in our own families? By what means will we show the love of God to those who are hurting?

So often we want things to be on our terms, "my way or the highway." This, my friend, is way above our pay grade. We cannot muscle or strong-arm our way out of the places we find ourselves in. Our child is acting in the agency God has freely given them. We don't always like it. We feel powerless, often alone and isolated. We are all ratifying our testimony—the end, dear ones, is in the hands of God. Let us not fight battles with the arm of flesh, which is brutal and unforgiving. Even in places where we differ or do not understand, may we come in the spirit of Jesus, with biblical humility. May we not act in ways the world tells us to, nor the religious church, but rather take a gamble on the love of God, which is so much deeper than anything we have to offer. Prayerfully releasing all of our children into the very best heaven has for them, we say, "Not my will but Yours be done," a prayer Jesus prayed in a garden oh, so long ago, one that can be echoed in our hearts and minds. A prayer of surrender where we let God define the ways in which our cries will be answered.

I often pray for God's best for my kids. His highest, the best He has for them, His perfect will for their lives. It has been said "the devil is in the details." I would rather leave the fine print to the Master of the universe and let Him work His plan, that which is beautiful in His sight.

If you have stuck with me thus far, you will realize that the "rightness" or "wrongness" of our child's choices are beyond the scope of this volume. We are called to land in love. There is a tendency that goes along with the human condition of going from A to Z in a heartbeat. We want speedy answers and a succinct end to the distress we are facing, we want the episode to be over in an hour. With the news of the way your child feels, we might think your whole world is falling apart. This is just not true! There are worse things in the universe…ask my friends who buried their son, the ones whose daughter died of a drug overdose, my daughter and her husband who gave birth to a stillborn child. What those families would do to face what we are facing! We get to love the children God has entrusted to our care, just as they are. Homosexuality is not the worst thing. There are losses beyond compare that we haven't even considered. Yes, we grieve loss in that our reality is different than what we thought was our ideal. Our image, what we imagined to be true, is not quite what we perceived. Ours is a journey of adjusting, rolling with a different version of the idyllic facts we have held dear and maybe even preached to others. Ours is not the loss of a child who went to heaven long before our hearts were ready, it is a realignment of thinking before the throne, asking for His heart for our child going forward.

Life is about choosing. Our children make choices every day. We too make decisions that affect the family dynamic. We agree with our kids on some things and not on others. God designed us with a free will. Whether we believe we do or not, we still categorize sin. For us to say we have gotten over one child living with their boyfriend or girlfriend but that we just can't get over this homosexuality stuff is an inconsistency that is ours to deal with. What sins are acceptable and what are not? Heterosexual acting out seems to be given a lesser penalty in the line-up of life. What about pornography? Are we dabbling in one thing while we condemn another?

We like life neat and tidy. We want the 'i's dotted and the 't's crossed. This is not that. We cannot "fix" this, it is not something for us to try and control. What we can do, like God does for us, is respect the child's right to make choices and invite them to continue in the beauty of a loving relationship going forward. Jumping to conclusions about their lifestyle or into "fix it" mode, laying blame, trying to analyze, therapize, or explain things away is not what is needed in these moments, which is taking care of the "log in our own eye," doing our own work. Laying aside ego or performance-oriented thinking, we battle for the hearts of our children.

We wrestle for the heart of our children on our knees, not in the court of public opinion. Mercy always triumphs over judgment. Many of us are left in shock when our child comes out as gay. Wherever we land, be it shock, grief, anger, or something else, let the feelings be felt but not directed at our kid as we navigate this our new reality. Misplaced feelings will serve no good purpose but to drive our kids further away from us and the dialogue we want to have with them.

Realize that we are not alone in our pursuit of sorting through the realities we are faced with. It is also true that generations to come will look at what we are tackling, shake their heads, and smile with how small this is in the big picture of things. Back in the day we worried about teen pregnancy, and while we never want to condone underage intercourse, if a child gets pregnant out of wedlock in this day and age, we don't take them outside and stone them, or at least I sincerely hope we don't!

Dads especially want to "come up with a plan"! Loving our children and protecting them from the dangers out there in the world is how we have managed so far, but this strategy is failing us in the here and now. Plan to pray for your kids and for those they love. Plan to love them, speak the truth in love, and keep reaching out to their hearts rather than driving them away from their sense of home and safety. Our question needs to be "How can we keep the lines of communication open?" rather than "How can I shut down a behavior?" Recognizing that they too might have questions going forward, may we all find safe community with which to wrangle out the many realities we might face. Maybe we have assigned blame for where we now are, husbands blaming wives, wives husbands, the school, the church. It is so much easier to blame someone else than lay this at the feet of Jesus, surrender the outcome and move forward in love. Fault-finding, judgment, and prejudice are all love-busters and will never win you good friends or create a better relationship with your kin. Let's be parents who don't leave a love vacuum for others to fill.

Churches don't typically know what to do with the LGBTQ community, where to put them. Christian kids who want a church family are often disappointed and have been affected by how inept we are with Jesus' mandate to love. It's as if there is an unwritten commandment, "Love everyone but these..." Let's not be the ones who don't reach out. Those who are afraid of the "gay in our midst" would do well to remember that they don't have a leprous disease but that each individual is an eternal soul that Jesus died for to draw them into the beauty of relationship with Him. As I am writing this, I am reminded of how Jesus treated those who did have leprous diseases, how He entered people's lives and left a legacy of love, touch, and healing in them. I want to be like Jesus. I believe you do too, or you wouldn't have read this far.

Pastor, parents, how many gay kids have you actually engaged with? Do you have a personal, loving, caring relationship with this community that such a lot of opinions are voiced about? Have you ever had a conversation with a gay individual? Often our arguments are theoretical in nature, they don't have skin on. We rail against the nameless, the faceless. Except this is not just an epic debate, this is a reality that affects real people with hearts and souls that matter! We are talking about people here. Cherished sons and daughters.

We have already established that we don't see eye to eye with our kids over every issue. My prayer is that we can come to the table with our progeny knowing even though we cannot totally agree, we can lay down our swords in the name of love, namely the love of God.

The diarrhea of popular opinion is everywhere. Care must be taken with who can speak into our lives (parent and child alike), with who will help form our thoughts at this turbulent time in our family history. We don't want to just take for granted that what we have been told will hold up in the courts of heaven, especially if what we have been spoon-fed down the ages is devoid of the love Jesus came to share. Person to person, human to human, spirit to spirit, we come inviting dialogue. What can we learn from one another? How can we move forward in His love, remembering that some things are more important than the "gay debate"?

15

CONCLUSIONS

One of the ways I pray is for God to remember miracles He has done in the past. I ask the Lord to remember some of His fine followers who have chosen the cross over culture, the Christ life over that of rampant desire. I ask the Lord to remember my friends who have struggled well with the Father for the lives of freedom they lead, and I ask Him to remember my boy: "Lord, remember this one, remember that one, remember my boy... God, what you have done for one, remember my son, my daughter."

We can pray for Jesus to meet directly with our kids, for God to do a deep and lasting work in their hearts. We can pray that He might send the right people into their lives to speak truth and life, that they hear what the Spirit is saying and respond well to Him.

We have to get rid of the notion that what we do is who

we are. Our feelings are real, but they are not always reality. What we do does not necessarily define who we are. What we feel is not always real! May we be those who call forth the identity of Jesus in our son or daughter. "I do this, so I am ..." does not always ring true. Who does He say that we are? Who does He say our kids are? I am going to speak His truth over my boy, how about you?

In the parable of the prodigal family, when the son came home, the Father put his robe over the rags. Daddy Prodigal met his son where he was at, covering the shame, the rags, not with his rage but with love that clothed and covered.

There is such a thing as speaking life over situations, calling the things that are not as though they are, telling the truth over a situation and watching God bring it to pass. We have seen Jesus change habits and hang-ups as His truth is chosen.

Pray the Word, not leaning on your doctrine or theology but praying the personal Word of God to your heart. Throughout the physical, progressive healing of my son, it was a moment-by-moment reliance on the One Who is able, literally leaning on the written Word, believing that the God who spoke was capable of doing that which He said. I couldn't lean on my understanding—I didn't understand, and what little I could comprehend told a very gloomy tale. I took to the Word and let my God do the work He promised therein. This was not a cotton candy kind of faith, light and fluffy with no substance. This was a desperate mother asking for the Word of the Lord to come to pass over her son's life. Our God Who has called us can bring His Word and will to pass!

Let us look for His glory within our story. What are we thanking God for as we tread this path? Where do we see His fingerprints, the marks He leaves behind as He calls us to follow Him on this walk of faith?

Culture is at war with Christian values. This is a time when our kids need us more than any other. We are being called to stand, sometimes, against preferences but never against people. Christians have become famous for the hate…this is not the Jesus way! Jesus would be found in the square with the LGBTQ+ community. He would go there, and I can only imagine the conversation that would be had! Jesus would go to that square to converse, not convert. We have pushed people away with our attitudes —isn't it time that we drew them close with our love? Have we by our actions shown those who struggle in our pews that they are not safe in the church, that they will never be truly loved or valued within the walls of their faith family? Have we given kids the message that they need to find true love and value outside of the family of God because we don't have the capacity for them, or that our Christianity can't cope with their choices? Preston Sprinkle says in *People to be Loved*, "People will gravitate to where they are loved the most. And if the world out-loves the church, then we have implicitly nudged our children away from the loving arms of Christ." God forbid!

Many of us were raised with shame—a well-oiled phrase in my childhood home was "Shame on you." Jesus never uses shame to bring us to change. He loves us into our new lives. He loves us, speaks truth over us, invites us, and woos us. We need to lose the contempt-colored lens through which we have viewed the world and stop imposing it on others.

Growth is often a painful process, but in this journey, we have a unique opportunity to enlarge our hearts in the unconditional love of God. Will we grow together?

I realize that, for some, this book is possibly not blunt enough against the gay lifestyle. For others, it will stir up deep feelings. May you have the grace to go where the feelings that are being aroused demand you go. May we, in humility, go to the Master, the Author and Finisher of our faith, and ask Him to hold and heal our hearts that we might respond as He would as we do His work of love in this world.

Maybe you felt blindsided in the process of your finding out how your child feels. Possibly you pushed your kid away. It is time to reclaim the closeness, to rebuild the trust that has been damaged. Affirm that "We are not throwing you or our relationship away." Things may look differently going forward, but what we want is to find our new normal. We probably don't understand, so we need to ask questions. Ask your child questions, ask the Lord, invite Him into the process as you journey on. May we at all times communicate with respect, remembering the mandate to love.

Feelings are not always facts. Our feelings frequently change. We are transformed in His Presence. Let us meet our kids where they are at, that they might know safety as they relate to us as parents.

Are there patterns in us that need to be surrendered, where we need to grow? Anger, rage, fear, anxiety—how will He heal us in this season as we follow Him on the journey we find ourselves on?

I have a friend who said, "When my kid came out, I had to too." There was no more space for hiding in the shadows of respectable churchianity, they had to own their new truth that their child was gay. Dodging the bullets of man's opinion is something we might have to get used to. We probably will have some vitriol hurled our way. Not everyone in the church can be trusted with our truth, nor will they always be kind. Repercussions will be felt, so why are we so surprised at our gay kids not feeling safe in the community of faith when we are tempted to tiptoe around the sensibilities of fellow believers?

For some readers, this effort will not be bold enough, not punchy enough against a lifestyle. But this volume is not about a lifestyle, it is about people with eternal souls.

Maybe you are a pastor reading this, I hope there are spiritual leaders who will read to lead well for families facing big challenges to their faith. Self-righteousness and what we might feel is religious or righteous indignation is a sin, my friends. What does He require of me in this season? We are not always aware of the way people are reacting in the pews one to another. We can't protect people from "stupid," but we don't have to model it from our pulpits either!

Sprinkle says in *People to be Loved*, "If a gay has the courage to come to our church, we better love them when they get there." Pastor friends, fellow followers of Jesus, we have a divine mandate on our lives to walk this out.

My son, my post-vasectomy child, has been a miracle from the beginning. He was God's idea, a sacred entrusting to our hearts and home. He has survived the hell of being run over by a dump truck (a saying we often use without full understanding). He was a miracle then and remains one still. My little rainbow guy.

> *"I set my rainbow in the cloud and it shall be a token or sign of a covenant or solemn pledge between me and the earth. And it shall be that when I bring clouds over the earth and the rainbow is seen in the clouds, I will earnestly remember my covenant or solemn pledge which is between me and you."*
>
> — GENESIS 9:13–15 AMP

Lord, bring back our rainbow revelation! May our covenant-keeping God go to work in the lives of our family as we parent the rainbow children we have been blessed with.

Believe me, when your child is in crisis, it is not their sexual identity that is the primary thought going through your mind. In a life-or-death situation, who he or she loves is not the biggest blip on the radar, it is that we long for life, for our kids to make it, to live to see another day.

Your life may be panning out differently than you originally thought it would. Will we do the work required for long-term relationship and connection? Many of us agree that we want our child in our lives, even if life as we knew it has changed forever. How do we want our stories to end? Do we want the volume we are living to be one of connection or contention? Everyone runs their own race, The Message says, "Run to win" (1 Corinthians 9:24 MSG). Run to win the heart of your child, not leaning on our limited understanding of how things should be, how we wish they were, but leaning into Jesus and His truth over the life of our family.

When Ethan was laying in his hospital bed hooked up to life support, I didn't assume I had the right answers or the right faith. I looked with desperation to the One Who holds life in His hands and asked what I could ask for, how I could pray. If we pray the prayers of heaven, we might be surprised at our intercession. God gave me Scripture to pray over our boy, whose life hung in the balance. Not one of those Scriptures had to do with same sex attraction… With deep gratitude to God, I get to love on my gay son today. He was given back to us in spite of the fact that on that awful day he was left for dead on the side of the road like a piece of garbage. My precious son is not garbage to God! I treasure the gift of his life with my Heavenly Father.

May we pray the prayers of heaven and do the fine work of continuing to love well the lambs He has entrusted us.

"Just love everyone. I'll sort them out later."— God

ALLISON ZIMMERMAN

"Beloved, let us love one another, for love is of God, and everyone who loves is born of God and knows God…"

— 1 JOHN 4:7

AFTERWORD

ROB ZIMMERMAN

When Allison and I got married in 1984, our hearts were overflowing with love for each other, and we were filled with faith and vision that our dreams would all come true. Life brings a whole new kind of reality as we encounter our share of experiences, good, bad, and sometimes ugly. But we saw ourselves as people of the Word, committed to traditional Christian family values. As our love blossomed even more, children started coming—five, in fact. I guess I may have envisioned something of a fantasy, that if we tried doing everything "right" in our life, our kids would grow up perfectly according to the standards we caught a glimpse of in our Bible-believing community. Never did I ever consider receiving that Facebook message from our son on 12/13/14 that he was gay. What did that even mean? How could that even be?!

I guess one aspect of my own life journey that I needed to face was the fear of negative consequences I might experience being a missionary with a gay son. I know this is not about me, but I admit I had some anxious thoughts of how this new reality might impact our career as ordained ministers. I had worked with denominations that often ostracized families who, if there was a divorce or a teenage pregnancy in the home, might fire or quietly retire the minister. To be honest, I think churches are guilty of creating the "cancel culture" that is rife today, shaming and shunning those we don't agree with, or worse, condemning the whole extended family for the individual decision a son or daughter may make. Sadly, Christians often face their toughest challenges in isolation because religious folks still seem to be more into public stonings, than compassionate care.

I'm so grateful God does not categorically reject us when we make the various choices that we do. Like depression or some other emotional state of being, homosexuality is not a simple feeling nor choice born out of rebellion to the will of God or biblical precepts. There are so many complex layers of personality and spirituality interacting in the person. God comes near us when we need healing. He does not cancel us as contagiously malignant even when we make certain choices. His love is long-suffering, and His kind of supernatural love makes miracles happen too! While physical addiction may have resulted from a decision to sample a particular drug, addiction as a matter of the heart never ends by "just saying no." Only divine loving-kindness expressed in unconditional ways over and over again is what keeps drawing us to the Savior, not shame, rejection, or Bible quotes.

Allison does an excellent job unpacking the musings of her own heart as we have moved forward from the lightning bolt that hit us on our Sunday drive. Her challenge to all of us to keep loving well, both our children and the gay community Ethan joined, is one that causes us to draw more deeply on the grace that is only found in the presence of Jesus, where His love covers everything, especially all the contradictions we may encounter as time goes on. His grace remains sufficient even today and tomorrow, no matter what we will experience. I still have questions swirling in my heart, but it is in these questions that, when I quiet my emotions and take time to bring them to God, the Lord personally draws near to speak into my life and reveal to me new glimpses of His love and glory. I am reminded that He is our Savior, and I am glad that is not my job. I can trust the Lord and His timing while I endeavor to be Ethan's dad who loves him well and always stays present, welcoming him with open arms.

This is how we continue in our journey with Ethan. We are for him, not against him as we pray the Word, recalling the many promises God has spoken over his life. Our faith is bolstered by the many miracles that God has performed in his life from the day he was conceived until now. Where people see the contradictions, we tenaciously cling to God and His Word.

AUTHOR NOTE

Dear Reader

Thank you for sticking with me thus far. I realize that this book has the potential to inflame and cause big feelings. Most of us are not neutral on the topic of Parenting the Rainbow.

There is a world of hurt out there and we the Church have been guilty of passing on the pain of generations.

May we continue to love like Christ and extend His love to those around us.

Thank you for reading these pages and as I write am praying for whatever reason you picked up this book in the first place.

Please feel free to leave a review and reach out personally if I can be of service at ajzwrites@gmail.com

Sincerely,
Allison

DISCUSSION QUESTIONS

Chapter 1

1. Can I value that this is not an easy process for parent or child?
2. How can I support those that might need it?
3. What is the Holy Spirit saying to my heart as I ponder these things?
4. Are there areas for me to grow in as I struggle or offer support to others?

Chapter 2

1. What does the fight for love look like in my context?
2. How will I continue to value my son/daughter?
3. Will I trust my child's future to God?

4. What does the path of mercy look like in my situation?

Chapter 3

1. How can I keep the lines of communication open in my relationship with my child?
2. How and where do I need to grow?
3. In an ideal dialogue, what would I want to be able to say?
4. Does my child coming out challenge who we are as a family?
5. Can I love enough to disagree without us rejecting one another?

Chapter 4

1. What do I believe, and does our child's narrative change my opinion?
2. In a sea of doubt, what will I believe God for?
3. What has our "table talk" been—loving and kind or judgmental and condemning?
4. How do I navigate loving through unfamiliar territory?
5. What is my normal reaction when hearing things I don't like? Shutting down, withdrawing, avoiding? Is this helpful?

DISCUSSION QUESTIONS

Chapter 5

1. In what ways can I reach out in love toward my child?
2. What is God saying to me in this season?
3. Who can I share the burdens and fears of my heart with in this season?
4. Have I typically used shame as a weapon to make people conform to my ideals?

Chapter 6

1. How can I bridge the divide of isolation and offer community to others?
2. What inner work do I need to do to become a true bridge for those who feel so alone?
3. How can I be more inclusive to those who think differently than me?
4. Am I willing to let God use me to reach out and genuinely love those in the gay community?

Chapter 7

1. Am I a safe person for someone to bring their struggles/truth to?
2. What is God saying to my heart in this season?
3. Is our God big enough to handle the things we currently face?
4. Am I someone God can use to make a difference in the situation I am facing?

5. Do I feel the need to control, or can I leave the outcome with God?

Chapter 8

1. How does my heart of love need to grow in this season?
2. Can I live in the tension of this discussion without becoming tense?
3. What strengths do I bring to the dialogue?
4. What weaknesses do I need to be aware of?

Chapter 9

1. Do my current reactions reflect His image?
2. How can I love well as I walk with my child/friend?
3. What are the prayers of the Spirit for your child?

Chapter 10

1. What is God asking of me in this season?
2. Are there lonely gay kids in my church community? If so, how can I genuinely care for their hearts?

Discussion Questions

Chapter 11

1. Does my current thinking match Calvary love?
2. Do we only see the mess, or do we have faith as the "message" is being unveiled?
3. Am I willing to be a listening ear rather than a source of judgment?

Chapter 12

1. What is being dredged up in me as I grapple with my child's sexuality?
2. How can we grow as a family to operate with mutual respect?
3. How can I continue to walk well on this path I find myself on?

Chapter 13

1. Where do I land concerning attending the wedding of a same sex couple?
2. If I have a spouse, do we differ?
3. If we differ, how will we proceed?
4. How open is my heart to being in relationship with those my child is in relationship with?

DISCUSSION QUESTIONS

Chapter 14

1. Am I committed to love for the long haul, regardless of outcome?
2. How can I be like Jesus as I pursue the heart of my child?
3. Is my church home a safe place for all, not just those who believe like I do?

RECOMMENDATIONS FOR FURTHER READING

Redeeming Sex: Naked Conversations About Sexuality and Spirituality, Debra Hirsch. Inter-Varsity Press.

People To Be Loved: Why Homosexuality Is Not Just an Issue, Preston M. Sprinkle. Zondervan.

ACKNOWLEDGMENTS

They say "it takes a village to raise a child." Truth be told, it takes one to raise a book from dream to reality.

With the utmost of gratitude, I have to thank my son Ethan. What you now hold was his idea. Ethan called forth a vision.

Rob, my husband, who always has a plethora of suggestions and vision galore!

My children—Ashley Marie, Heather Grace, Shannon Rose, and Josiah Robert, along with Ethan Treue—you have shaped this story with your indomitable love and courage, and your spouses, Leana Rae, De'Andrew, and Amir, all of whom have their own iteration of love and generosity as we embrace our rainbow.

Lyle and Ronda Wells, who have their own love story to tell, let me into their world and the ways they have shown up with courage and kindness.

Rich Bullock, whose friendship and expertise have been a constant gift. Without his part, what we now hold would still be taking up space in my humble iPad.

Linda Rowett, whose idea it was to include questions as a way to process the contents of *Parenting the Rainbow*.

Pash, we hashed out the title together, and I am ever grateful for the privilege to be in your life.

GayMarie Vaughan for invaluable insight.

Nathan Edwardson for continuing to champion the call of God on my life and making space for the stories I have to tell.

Trevor and Diane Hill, who selflessly gave space for me to finish this volume as a guest in their home.

John and Joy West for the gift of their cottage to finish the final draft.

Robert Holden for his editing prowess and tender handling of what we now hold.

Courageous people of the former Zion Fellowship, Guam, thanks for loving us well and allowing us the space to own what was to become ours without judgment.

Lynn for being a very present part in this and other chapters yet to be told.

Anne Shannon, who graciously gave into conversation around *Parenting the Rainbow*.

Others whose names are not mentioned but who are an unforgettable part of this project.

ABOUT THE AUTHOR

Allison Zimmerman, mother of five, grandmother of nine, along with her husband Rob has spent the majority of her life story in the Pacific islands. In 2015 she was called away from the lands she loved to care for her son, who had been crushed and left for dead in a hit and run. Her son continues to make a miraculous recovery.

Allison is an engaging speaker who wraps truth in humor. Her dependence on the Word of God and the God of the Word has kept her heart and soul in hard places.

Good People, also written by Allison, a children's book, helps families have a voice against childhood sexual abuse.

Allison is available to minister and can be reached at ajzwrites@gmail.com

ALSO BY ALLISON ZIMMERMAN

Good People

This is a must-have in our efforts to protect the children in our world from childhood sexual abuse and exploitation.

Printed in Great Britain
by Amazon

87468756R00081